Better Homes and Gardens®

GOURMET RECIPES
Made Easy

© 1980 by Meredith Corporation, Des Moines, Iowa.
All Rights Reserved. Printed in the United States of America.
First Edition. First Printing.
Library of Congress Catalog Card Number: 79-53042
ISBN: 0-696-00525-5

On the cover: End an elegant meal with flaming *Crêpes Suzette* (see recipe, page 75).

BETTER HOMES AND GARDENS® BOOKS

Editor: Gerald M. Knox
Art Director: Ernest Shelton

Food and Nutrition Editor: Doris Eby
Senior Associate Food Editor: Sharyl Heiken
Senior Food Editors: Sandra Granseth,
    Elizabeth Woolever
Associate Food Editors: Mary Cunningham,
    Joanne Johnson, Bonnie Lasater, Marcia Stanley,
    Joy Taylor, Pat Teberg
Recipe Development Editor: Marion Viall
Test Kitchen Director: Sharon Golbert
Test Kitchen Home Economists: Jean Brekke,
    Kay Cargill, Marilyn Cornelius,
    Maryellyn Krantz, Marge Steenson

Associate Art Directors: Randall Yontz,
    Neoma Alt West
Copy and Production Editors: David Kirchner,
    Lamont Olson, David Walsh
Assistant Art Director: Harijs Priekulis
Senior Graphic Designer: Faith Berven
Graphic Designers: Linda Ford,
    Sheryl Veenschoten, Tom Wegner

Editor-in-Chief: James A. Autry
Editorial Director: Neil Kuehnl
Group Administrative Editor: Duane Gregg
Executive Art Director: William J. Yates

Gourmet Recipes Made Easy
Editors: Joy Taylor, Elizabeth Woolever
Copy and Production Editor: David Kirchner
Graphic Designer: Harijs Priekulis

Our seal assures you that every recipe in
Gourmet Recipes Made Easy is endorsed
by the Better Homes and Gardens Test Kitchen.
Each recipe is tested for family appeal,
practicality, and deliciousness.

Contents

Welcome to Gourmet Cooking

Beef Wellington. Oysters Rockefeller. Eggs Benedict. Baked Alaska. No longer are these specialties reserved for restaurant dining — now you can learn to prepare them at home. We've taken the mystery out of preparing these and many other exciting gourmet foods. Photographs that detail unfamiliar techniques accompany every recipe, sharing with you the "secrets" of these classic foods. These are recipes you'll start with confidence and complete with success.

You may be surprised to find that some gourmet recipes are simple and elegant while others are quite elaborate. And not all gourmet foods are difficult or expensive to prepare. Gourmet cooking is simply a blending of ingredients and techniques that makes a food special. In the following pages you'll discover a variety of recipes — from toothsome appetizers to sinfully rich desserts—around which you can plan an entire gourmet meal. Menu Suggestions appear throughout the book. And on the last page of each section, you'll find special recipes to use with a variety of gourmet foods. These include Beef Stock, Chicken Stock, Béchamel Sauce, Hollandaise Sauce, Mayonnaise, Flavored Butters, and Dessert Coffees.

Refer to the "Garnishes" section for a variety of attractive garnishes you can make to enhance your gourmet meals. In our "Basic Techniques" section, we've assembled information on several cooking methods and equipment uses that pertain to many types of recipes. And check "Appliance Shortcuts" for hints on how to make preparing gourmet recipes even easier with your microwave oven and food processor.

Acquaint yourself with *Gourmet Recipes Made Easy* and discover how easy it is to prepare delicious, attractive foods.

Planning Gourmet Meals

Preparing a gourmet meal can be relaxing and rewarding if you take the time to plan ahead. Don't plunge into a seven-course extravaganza if this is your first attempt at gourmet cooking. Instead, plan an elegant meal around one (or two) special recipes. You'll feel more confident concentrating your first efforts on just a couple recipes that involve unfamiliar techniques.

Choose easy yet elegant foods to accompany your gourmet fare. For instance, prepare a steamed vegetable and top it with a special sauce, such as Hollandaise Sauce. Or serve a flavored butter with the dinner rolls. For dessert, spoon your favorite liqueur over ice cream. A little extra effort turns a plain food into something special!

Throughout this book, you'll find many Menu Suggestions that feature no-fuss, elegant foods to round out a single gourmet entrée. But don't be limited by our ideas; create personalized menus to satisfy your own tastes and talents. As you gain expertise in gourmet cooking, you can plan meals around several gourmet recipes, or even serve an all-gourmet dinner.

When planning a gourmet meal (or any meal), keep in mind that it should be nutritious, attractive, and, of course, delicious! Try to serve foods that complement each other in flavor, texture, and color.

Accent a bland food with a full-flavored sauce. Present a light dessert after a heavy meal, and a rich dessert after lighter fare. And serve foods with a pleasing variety of shapes and temperatures. Remember, you are creating a picture at the dinner table that consists of the table setting and the food. Be sure to include garnishes that will enhance the total effect.

Wine can make a gourmet meal even more special. A carefully chosen bottle of wine ties together all elements of the meal, and adds a special elegance of its own. Choose an appropriate wine after you've planned the menu, and refer to these guidelines.

Generally, white dinner wines, which are dry and light in flavor and either tart or full-bodied, taste best with lighter foods such as veal, poultry, and seafood. Red dinner wines, which usually are dry and rich, are a good match for beef, spicy foods, and heartier fare. Rosé wines, which are simply pale red wines that may be either sweet or dry, complement most any food.

These are only guidelines — not strict rules. Always chose the wine that suits your taste and at the same time complements your well-planned gourmet meal.

The first time around, you may want to prepare a gourmet recipe for close friends or family, who will be more than pleased to taste the results of your cooking adventures. If you have friends who share your interest in gourmet cooking, consider starting a gourmet dinner group. It's a delightful way to savor good food in the company of friends who appreciate each others' gourmet endeavors. After some experimenting and taste-testing, you'll be ready to impress some very special dinner guests with your gourmet skills.

Meats

Beef, veal, lamb, and pork are given the star treatment they deserve in the recipe pages that follow. *Pork Stir-Fry* is made with a variety of colorful Oriental vegetables and served atop *Deep-Fried Rice Sticks* (see recipes, page 13). Rich pastry encloses a tender beef tenderloin and a liver pâté mixture for elegant *Beef Wellington* (see recipe, pages 10 and 11). And a mushroom sauce tops broiled *Wild Rice-Stuffed Chops* (see recipe, page 9).

Veal Marsala

Veal, the young, tender meat of a calf, is widely used by Italy's cooks. Veal Marsala and Veal Piccata are simple examples of how Italians prepare this delicate meat for a delicious meal—

- **1 pound veal leg round steak *or* sirloin steak, cut ¼ inch thick**
- **3 tablespoons butter *or* margarine**
- **½ cup water**
- **¼ cup marsala *or* dry sherry**
- **1 teaspoon instant chicken bouillon granules**
- **1 4-ounce can sliced mushrooms, drained**
- **1 tablespoon snipped parsley**

Cut veal into 4 pieces. Place 1 piece of veal between 2 pieces of clear plastic wrap. Pound with meat mallet to about ⅛-inch thickness, working from center to edges (see photo). Remove plastic wrap; sprinkle with salt and pepper. Repeat with remaining veal. In large skillet cook *half* of the veal in hot butter or margarine over medium-high heat about 1 minute on each side. Remove to serving platter; keep warm. Add a little more butter or margarine, if necessary. Repeat with remaining veal. Keep veal warm. Add water, marsala or dry sherry, and bouillon granules to drippings in skillet. Boil rapidly 3 to 4 minutes or till liquid is reduced to about ⅓ cup. Stir in sliced mushrooms and parsley. Pour over veal. Serve immediately. Makes 4 servings.

Veal Piccata

Prepare Veal Marsala as above *except* omit the water, marsala or dry sherry, bouillon granules, and mushrooms. Cook veal as above. To skillet drippings add 3 tablespoons *lemon juice*, 2 tablespoons *butter or margarine*, and the 1 tablespoon snipped parsley. Heat and stir till butter melts; pour over veal. Garnish with lemon slices, if desired.

Place veal between two pieces of clear plastic wrap to prevent perforating the meat. Using the fine-toothed side of a meat mallet, pound each piece of veal to ⅛-inch thickness, working from center to edges. If a meat mallet is not available, pound the veal with the flat side of a chef's knife or cleaver.

Menu Suggestion

Accompany Veal Piccata with other Italian specialties for a true ethnic meal.

Veal Piccata
Saffron Risotto
(see recipe, page 70)

Green beans with almonds   Breadsticks
Spumoni

Wild Rice-Stuffed Chops

A rich mushroom sauce tops these broiled pork chops, pictured on pages 6 and 7—

- ¼ **cup wild rice**
- ¾ **cup water**
- 3 **tablespoons dry sherry**
- ¾ **cup chopped fresh mushrooms**
- 3 **tablespoons chopped onion**
- ½ **teaspoon salt**
- ¼ **teaspoon pepper**
- ¼ **teaspoon ground sage**
- 2 **tablespoons butter** *or* **margarine**
- ¼ **cup chopped almonds**
- 6 **pork loin rib chops, cut 1½ inches thick (4 pounds)**
- ¼ **cup sliced fresh mushrooms**
- 2 **tablespoons chopped onion**
- 2 **tablespoons butter** *or* **margarine**
- 2 **teaspoons cornstarch**
- ⅛ **teaspoon dry mustard**
- 1 **cup Beef Stock (see recipe, page 19)**

Run cold water over wild rice in a strainer for 1 to 2 minutes, lifting rice with fingers. In saucepan combine wild rice, ¾ cup water, and sherry. Bring to boiling; reduce heat. Cover and simmer about 40 minutes or till rice is tender. Drain, if necessary. Meanwhile, in skillet cook ¾ cup chopped mushrooms, 3 tablespoons onion, salt, pepper, and sage in 2 tablespoons butter till onion is tender but not brown. Remove from heat. Stir in wild rice and almonds.

Make a pocket in each chop by cutting from fat side almost to bone edge (step 1). Lightly spoon ¼ cup of the wild rice mixture into each chop (step 2). Close the opening with wooden picks (step 3). Place stuffed chops on unheated rack of broiler pan. Broil chops 5 inches from heat about 18 minutes. Sprinkle chops lightly with salt and pepper. Turn chops and broil 18 minutes more or till chops are done.

Meanwhile, prepare sauce. In saucepan cook ¼ cup sliced mushrooms and 2 tablespoons chopped onion in 2 tablespoons butter till tender. Stir in cornstarch, dry mustard, ⅛ teaspoon *salt*, and dash *pepper*. Add Beef Stock all at once. Cook and stir till thickened and bubbly. Cook 2 minutes more. Remove from heat. To serve, remove wooden picks from chops. Spoon sauce over. Serves 6.

1 Use a sharp knife to cut a 1½– to 2-inch-long slit in the fatty side of chop. Insert knife into slit, as shown, and draw it from side to side to form a larger pocket inside the chop, cutting almost to bone edge. Try not to make the first slit larger than 2 inches.

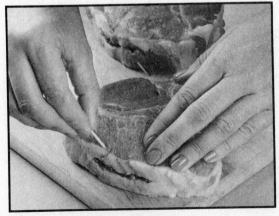

2 Using a tablespoon, lightly spoon about ¼ cup of the stuffing mixture into the pocket of each pork chop. The stuffing should not be tightly packed.

3 Securely close the pocket opening with 1 or 2 wooden picks inserted diagonally. This keeps the stuffing from falling out while the chops broil.

Beef Wellington

Pictured on pages 6 and 7—

1½ **cups chopped fresh mushrooms**
½ **cup chopped leek** *or* **onion**
2 **tablespoons butter** *or* **margarine**
½ **cup Chicken Liver Pâté (see recipe, page 26)** *or* **two 2¾-ounce cans liver pâté**
3 **tablespoons fine dry bread crumbs**
2 **tablespoons burgundy**
1 **2-pound beef tenderloin** *or* **beef eye round roast**
1½ **cups all-purpose flour**
½ **cup shortening**
3 **to 4 tablespoons water**
1 **tablespoon butter, softened**
1 **beaten egg**
¾ **cup Beef Stock (see recipe, page 19)**
2 **tablespoons all-purpose flour**
¼ **cup burgundy**
¼ **teaspoon dried basil, crushed**

Cook mushrooms and leek in 2 tablespoons butter till tender. Stir in Chicken Liver Pâté, crumbs, and 2 tablespoons burgundy. Cover and chill. Place beef on rack in shallow roasting pan. Insert meat thermometer. Roast in 425° oven for 35 to 45 minutes or till thermometer registers 130°. Remove from pan; cool. Reserve drippings.

For pastry, stir together 1½ cups flour and ¼ teaspoon *salt*. Cut in shortening till size of small peas. Add water, 1 tablespoon at a time, tossing with fork till all is moistened. Form into a ball. Set aside ⅛ of the pastry for the decorative cutouts. Roll the remainder into a 15x10-inch rectangle on a lightly floured surface. Spread *half* the softened butter over pastry. Fold dough crosswise into thirds (step 1). Spread remaining softened butter over pastry; fold crosswise into thirds (step 2).

Roll the folded pastry dough into a 15x10-inch rectangle on a floured surface. Spread pâté mixture over pastry to within ½ inch of the edges. Center meat atop. Overlap long sides (step 3). Brush edges with a little beaten egg; seal. Trim excess dough from ends; fold up. Brush with egg; seal. Place seam side down on greased baking sheet. Roll reserved dough; make cutouts (step 4). Place cutouts on meat (step 5); cover and chill 2 hours. Brush remain-

ing egg over pastry. Bake in 425° oven for 35 minutes or till pastry is golden. Heat reserved meat drippings with Beef Stock. Blend together 2 tablespoons flour and ¼ cup cold *water*; stir into hot mixture with ¼ cup burgundy and basil. Cook and stir till thickened. Season. Garnish with snipped parsley. Serves 6 to 8.

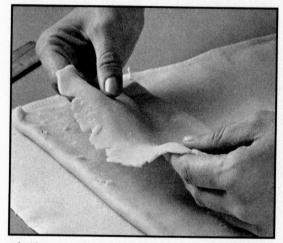

1 After spreading 1½ teaspoons of softened butter on the pastry, fold the pastry. Carefully lift the dough, without stretching, and fold it into thirds, as shown.

2 Spread another 1½ teaspoons of softened butter on the folded pastry. Again fold the dough into thirds, as shown. The softened butter adds a special richness to the pastry.

Menu Suggestion

This menu, designed for six people, includes easy-to-prepare foods so you can concentrate your efforts on the Beef Wellington. Prepare the sauce for the Poached Nectarines in advance and just reheat it at dessert time.

Beef Wellington

Baked potato

Spinach salad with Vinaigrette dressing

Poached Nectarines

(see recipe, page 76)

3 Center the meat atop the rolled-out pastry. Carefully lift up long edge, as shown, pressing against meat. Repeat with the remaining long edge, overlapping pastry atop meat. Brush edge with beaten egg; seal.

4 Roll out the reserved dough. Cut the dough into desired shapes such as flowers, leaves, hearts, or diamonds using a decorative cutter. (Or, cut the dough with a knife into ¾-inch strips and place these strips lattice-style on the pastry. This lattice-style on the Beef Wellington is pictured on pages 6 and 7.) Choose a design that fits the occasion.

5 Place the wrapped meat on the baking sheet, seam side down. Arrange the decorative cutouts atop the pastry. You can overlap the cutouts slightly, but excessive overlapping will cause uneven baking of the pastry.

11

Cider-Baked Ham

A brown sugar and ground clove mixture is patted on the ham to create a delicious crust—

- 1 **5– to 7-pound fully cooked ham, rump half**
- 4 **cups apple cider** *or* **apple juice**
- 2 **medium onions, quartered**
- 2 **tablespoons lemon juice**
- 1 **beaten egg**
- ⅓ **cup packed brown sugar**
- 1 **teaspoon ground cloves**
- ⅔ **cup raisins**
- ⅔ **cup orange marmalade**
- 1 **tablespoon lemon juice**
- 2 **tablespoons cornstarch**
- ¼ **teaspoon ground allspice**

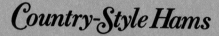

Country-Style Hams

These hams are specially processed to give them a distinctive flavor. They are dry-salt cured, sometimes smoked, and usually aged. Country-style hams have not been completely cooked during processing; bake them to an internal temperature of 160°. Follow label directions for scrubbing and soaking these hams.

Place ham, fat side up, on rack in shallow roasting pan. Score in diamonds (step 1). Combine apple cider or apple juice, onions, and 2 tablespoons lemon juice. Add to roasting pan. Bake in 325° oven for 1¾ hours. Brush the fat surface of the ham with the beaten egg. Combine brown sugar and ground cloves and pat onto the fat surface of the ham. Insert meat thermometer, making sure tip does not rest on bone or fat. Return ham to oven. Continue baking for 30 minutes or till thermometer registers 140°, basting ham occasionally with the cider mixture. Remove from oven. Transfer ham to serving platter and keep warm. Strain cider mixture; skim fat. Reserve 1 cup of the strained liquid. In saucepan combine raisins, the 1 cup apple cider mixture, and 1 cup *water*. Stir in marmalade and 1 tablespoon lemon juice. Combine cornstarch and allspice. Stir into raisin mixture. Cook and stir till bubbly; keep warm.

To carve ham, place cut side down on cutting board. Cut along bone from top to board to remove a large boneless piece (step 2). Place this boneless piece of ham cut side down on the cutting board and slice meat across the grain. To carve meat remaining on the bone, make horizontal slices (step 3). Serve warm sauce with ham. Serves 12.

1 Score ham fat using a sharp knife to make diagonal ¼-inch-deep cuts across ham in a diamond pattern. A paper strip makes a handy cutting guide, as shown.

2 To carve ham, place cut side down on cutting board. On one side of the ham is a boneless piece that can be cut away from the bone. Cut along the bone to remove this piece.

3 To carve meat remaining on the bone, insert fork into meat next to bone and make horizontal slices to the bone. Cut each slice away from the bone using the tip of the knife.

Pork Stir-Fry

Prepare all ingredients before you start to stir-fry. Pictured on pages 6 and 7 —

- **1 pound boneless pork**
- **⅓ cup soy sauce**
- **1 tablespoon cornstarch**
- **¼ cup Beef Stock (see recipe, page 19)**
- **2 tablespoons dry sherry**
- **½ teaspoon crushed red pepper**
- **4 dried mushrooms**
- **2 tablespoons cooking oil**
- **1 teaspoon grated gingerroot**
- **1 clove garlic, minced**
- **1 cup bias-sliced green onions**
- **1 cup thinly sliced carrots**
- **½ cup slivered almonds**
- **2 cups thinly sliced bok choy**
- **1 6-ounce package frozen pea pods, thawed**
- **1 cup fresh bean sprouts *or* ½ of a 16-ounce can bean sprouts, drained**
- **4 ounces fresh tofu (bean curd), cubed Deep-Fried Rice Sticks *or* hot cooked rice**

Partially freeze pork; slice very thinly across the grain into bite-size pieces (step 1). In small bowl blend soy sauce into cornstarch; stir in Beef Stock, dry sherry, and red pepper; set aside. Soak mushrooms in enough warm water to cover for 30 minutes; squeeze to drain well. Chop mushrooms, discarding stems; set aside.

Preheat a wok or large skillet over high heat. For gas ranges, place the wide end of the wok ring stand *down* over the largest burner and place wok in stand. For electric ranges, place the wide end of the wok ring stand *up* over the largest burner and place wok in stand. Add cooking oil to wok or skillet. Stir-fry gingerroot and garlic in hot oil for 30 seconds. Add green onions and carrots; stir-fry 1 minute. Add almonds and mushrooms; stir-fry 1 to 2 minutes. Remove from wok. (Add more oil to wok, if necessary.) Add bok choy to wok; stir-fry 1 minute. Add pea pods, bean sprouts, and tofu. Stir-fry 1 minute (step 2). Remove from wok. Add *half* the pork to hot wok or skillet; stir-fry 2 minutes. Remove pork. Stir-fry remaining pork 2 minutes. Return all pork to wok; push pork away from center of wok. Stir soy mixture; add to wok (step 3). Cook and stir until bubbly. Return all vegetables to wok. Cover; cook 1 minute or till heated through. Serve over Deep-Fried Rice Sticks or hot cooked rice. Makes 6 servings.

Deep-Fried Rice Sticks: Fry 2 ounces *unsoaked rice sticks*, a few at a time, in deep hot *cooking oil* (375°) about 5 seconds or just till sticks puff and rise to the top. Remove; drain on paper toweling. Keep warm in oven.

1 Thinly slice the meat across the grain into bite-size pieces using a sharp cleaver or knife, as shown. Partially freezing the meat makes it easier to slice into thin slices.

2 Use a long-handled spoon or spatula to stir-fry, as shown. Frequently lift and turn the food with a folding motion. Always use high heat so food cooks quickly.

3 Push pork away from center of wok. Then, add the soy-cornstarch mixture, as shown. Let mixture bubble slightly before stirring it into the pork. Cook and stir till thickened and bubbly.

Steak Tartare

Be sure to serve this dish within an hour of preparing the meat—

1 **pound boneless beef sirloin steak**
4 *to* 6 **egg yolks**
⅓ **cup snipped parsley**
⅓ **cup sliced green onion**
Condiments (choose any or all of the following): mustard, anchovy fillets, capers, pepper, salt, paprika, worcestershire sauce, bottled hot pepper sauce, dairy sour cream, caviar)
Toast points

Trim all gristle and fat from meat. Cut meat into ½-inch cubes. Spread the meat cubes in a single layer. Use two very sharp knives to finely chop the meat. With one knife in each hand, hold them very close to one another with blades parallel and tips crisscrossing slightly. Pull the knives away from one another, cutting through the meat (step 1). Meat will spread out as it is chopped. Push meat together (step 2) and continue cutting till meat is very finely chopped. (*Or*, grind the steak, half at a time, with food grinder or food processor.) Divide uncooked meat into four to six portions; shape into mounded patties on individual chilled plates. Make an indentation in the center of each patty; place an uncooked egg yolk in each indentation. Sprinkle parsley and onion atop meat (step 3); pass choice of condiments to sprinkle atop. Mix before eating. Serve with toast points. Makes 6 appetizer servings or 4 main dish servings.

1 Hold knives parallel and very close. Draw the knives away from one another, applying pressure, to cut through the meat, as shown.

2 Use both knives to push the chopped meat back into a compact single layer. Continue cutting the meat as in step 1, stopping frequently to push meat together.

3 Sprinkle snipped parsley and green onion atop the meat and egg yolk. Each diner then tosses their own meat, yolk, and choice of condiments with a fork before eating. If desired, the meat mixture can be spread on toast points.

Menu Suggestion

Enjoy Steak Tartare as an appetizer or main dish. The following menu is for a light meal. Prepare the dessert ahead of time.

Steak Tartare   Wilted spinach salad
Toast points *or* crisp crackers
Assorted relishes
Cherry Sorbet
(see recipe, page 86)

Sauerbraten with Spaetzle

Marinating the meat for 36 to 72 hours gives it a special flavor—

- ¾ **cup dry red wine**
- ¾ **cup red wine vinegar**
- 1 **medium onion, sliced**
- 1 **lemon, sliced**
- 1 **tablespoon sugar**
- 3 **whole black peppercorns, crushed**
- 2 **bay leaves**
- 8 **whole cloves**
- ¼ **teaspoon ground allspice**
- 1 **4-pound boneless beef round rump roast**
- 2 **tablespoons cooking oil**
- ½ **cup chopped onion**
- ½ **cup chopped carrot**
- ¼ **cup chopped celery**
  Spaetzle
- 1 **cup broken gingersnaps**
- ½ **cup fine dry bread crumbs**
- ¼ **cup butter** *or* **margarine, melted**

In large saucepan combine dry red wine, wine vinegar, onion slices, lemon, sugar, crushed peppercorns, bay leaves, cloves, allspice, 2½ cups *water,* and 1 tablespoon *salt.* Bring to boiling. Remove from heat; cool to room temperature. Place roast in large plastic bag; set in large bowl. Pour marinade into bag (step 1). Refrigerate 36 to 72 hours, turning bag occasionally to distribute marinade. Remove meat; wipe dry. Strain marinade; reserve.

In Dutch oven brown roast on all sides in hot oil. Add reserved marinade, chopped onion, carrot, and celery. Cover and simmer about 2 hours or till meat is tender. Meanwhile, prepare Spaetzle.

Transfer meat to platter; keep warm. Remove vegetables with slotted spoon. Reserve 2 cups of the liquid. Return vegetables and reserved liquid to Dutch oven; stir in gingersnaps and ⅔ cup *water.* Cook and stir till thickened and bubbly.

Combine fine dry bread crumbs and melted butter. Spoon over Spaetzle. Slice meat and arrange slices over Spaetzle; spoon some gravy over meat. Pass remaining gravy. Makes 8 to 10 servings.

1 *Place roast in large plastic bag, then set in a deep bowl for easier handling. Pour the marinade mixture over the meat in the bag. Close the bag; turn to distribute the marinade evenly over the meat.*

2 *Press batter through deep-fat frying basket or colander with ¼-inch holes with the back of a wooden spoon or rubber spatula. If dough is too thick to push through, thin it with a little milk.*

Spaetzle

Combine 2 cups *all-purpose flour* and 1 tablespoon *salt.* Mix 2 *eggs* and ¾ cup *milk;* stir into flour mixture. Place batter in coarse-sieved deep-fat frying basket or colander with ¼-inch holes. Hold over kettle of boiling salted water. Press batter through frying basket (step 2). Cook and stir for 5 minutes; drain. Keep warm.

Stuffed Leg of Lamb

1 5- to 6-pound boneless leg of lamb
¼ cup chopped onion
¼ cup chopped celery
1 tablespoon butter *or* margarine
2 cups dry bread cubes
¼ cup raisins
1 tablespoon finely shredded orange peel
¼ teaspoon ground cinnamon
1 beaten egg
⅓ cup packed brown sugar
2 tablespoons cornstarch
¾ teaspoon ground ginger
2 tablespoons snipped fresh mint leaves
    or 2 teaspoons dried mint flakes,
    crushed
1 tablespoon finely shredded orange peel
1¾ cups orange juice
2 tablespoons butter *or* margarine
2 oranges, peeled, sectioned, and cut up

Make 1 or 2 lengthwise slits in large muscles of lamb; do not cut completely through (step 1). Score meat diagonally about ¼ inch deep. Pound lamb between pieces of plastic wrap to ¾-inch thickness; sprinkle with salt and pepper. Cook onion and celery in 1 tablespoon butter till onion is tender. Toss with bread cubes, raisins, 1 tablespoon orange peel, cinnamon, and the egg. Spread stuffing over lamb; roll up jelly-roll style from short side (step 2). Secure with string both crosswise and lengthwise (step 3).

Insert spit rod lengthwise through center of rolled leg. Adjust holding forks (step 4); check for even balance. Prepare a foil drip pan (step 5); place in grill. Arrange *medium* coals around drip pan. Attach spit; position drip pan under meat. Test temperature of coals (step 6). Turn on motor; lower hood or cover spit rod with a foil tent. Roast over *medium* coals for 1¼ to 1½ hours for medium doneness or till a meat thermometer registers 160°. Remove from spit; keep warm.

For sauce, combine brown sugar, cornstarch, ginger, and 1 teaspoon *salt*. Stir in mint, 1 tablespoon orange peel, and orange juice. Place over *medium* coals or medium heat and cook till thickened and bubbly. Stir in 2 tablespoons butter and orange pieces. Remove strings from roast and slice meat. Spoon some sauce over and pass remainder. Serves 12.

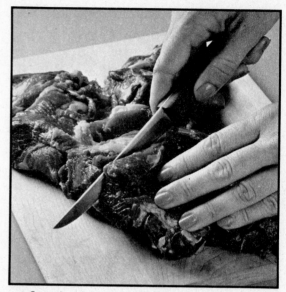

1 Spread out lamb on cutting board. Make 1 or 2 lengthwise slits in the large muscles, but do not cut meat all the way through. These slits should let the lamb lie flat for easier rolling.

2 Roll up the lamb jelly-roll style from the short side, tucking in any uneven edges. This keeps the stuffing intact and also prevents overcooking of any thin edges of meat. The meat roll should be neat and compact.

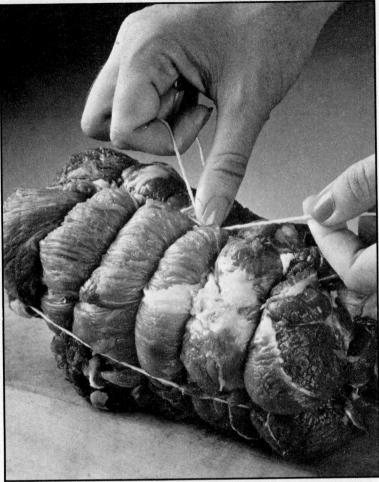

3 *Secure the meat roll with kitchen string. Tie it crosswise at several places, then tie it twice lengthwise. The string keeps the meat roll closed and holds the stuffing inside the meat during spit-roasting. Remove string to slice.*

Menu Suggestion

For a large dinner party, this menu allows advance preparation. Make the torte a day ahead of time, and prepare the Honey Butter and Romaine salad several hours in advance. For an extra touch, garnish each dinner plate with an orange twist and a sprig of mint.

Stuffed Leg of Lamb
Buttered steamed carrots
Romaine salad
Warm dinner rolls
Honey Butter
(see recipe, page 71)

Almond Torte
(see recipe, page 84)

4 *Insert spit rod lengthwise through center of the rolled leg. Secure with holding forks. Check for balance by holding one rod end in the palm of each hand and turning gently. If the meat turns unevenly, readjust the forks or rod.*

5 *For drip pan, tear off a piece of 18-inch-wide heavy-duty foil twice the length of grill; fold in half for a double thickness. Turn up all edges 1½ inches. Miter corners securely and fold tips toward the inside for added strength.*

6 *Test temperature of coals by holding hand about 4 inches above coals. Begin counting "one thousand one, one thousand two,...." If you need to withdraw your hand after 4 seconds, the coals are medium.*

17

Steak au Poivre
(Steak o PWAV-rah)

To impress dinner guests, prepare the steaks in a chafing dish at tableside—

- **2 teaspoons whole black peppercorns**
- **4 beef top loin steaks, cut 1 inch thick (2 pounds)**
- **2 tablespoons butter *or* margarine**
- **1 tablespoon olive oil *or* cooking oil**
- **¼ cup cognac *or* other brandy**
- **¼ cup Beef Stock (see recipe, page 19)**

Coarsely crack the peppercorns with mortar and pestle. Slash fat edge of steaks at 1-inch intervals. Sprinkle one side of each steak with ¼ teaspoon of the cracked peppercorns; rub over meat and press into surface (step 1). Repeat on other side of steaks. Let steaks stand at room temperature for 30 minutes.

In a 12-inch skillet or blazer pan of chafing dish, heat butter with olive oil. Cook steaks over medium-high heat to desired doneness, turning once. (Allow 12 minutes total cooking time for medium doneness.) Season steaks with salt.

Add cognac or brandy to skillet, pouring over steaks. Carefully ignite (step 2); allow flames to subside. Remove steaks to hot platter; keep warm. Add Beef Stock to skillet. Bring to boiling; pour over steaks. Makes 4 servings.

1 Crack the peppercorns using a mortar and pestle or pepper mill. Sprinkle one side of steak with ¼ teaspoon of the cracked peppercorns; press into steak with fingertips. Repeat this procedure on both sides of steaks.

2 Pour cognac or brandy over steaks. Light a long match and hold over the skillet to ignite cognac. Extinguish match. Allow flames in skillet to subside, then remove steaks to hot platter.

Menu Suggestion

Flavorful Steak au Poivre should be served with lightly seasoned foods.

Steak au Poivre
Broccoli spears with Hollandaise Sauce
(see recipe, page 51)

Twice-baked potatoes
Vanilla ice cream with hot fruit sauce

Beef Stock

See the tip on page 29 for stock substitutes—

- **6 pounds meaty beef soup bones**
- **3 carrots, cut up**
- **1 large onion, sliced**
- **½ cup water**
- **2 stalks celery with leaves, cut up**
- **1 large tomato, cut up**
- **1 small head cabbage, cut up**
- **8 whole black peppercorns**
- **4 sprigs parsley**
- **1 bay leaf**
- **1 tablespoon salt**
- **2 teaspoons dried thyme, crushed**
- **1 clove garlic, halved**

In a large shallow roasting pan place soup bones, carrots, and onion. Bake the bones, uncovered, in a 450° oven about 30 minutes or till bones are well browned, turning occasionally. Drain off fat. In a 10-quart Dutch oven or kettle place the browned bones, carrots, and onion. Pour the water into roasting pan and rinse. Pour this liquid into Dutch oven. Add the celery, tomato, cabbage, peppercorns, parsley, bay leaf, salt, thyme, garlic and 12 cups *water*. Bring to boiling. Reduce heat; cover and simmer 5 hours. Strain stock. Discard meat, vegetables, and seasonings. Clarify stock, if desired (see Chicken Consommé, page 29, for directions). If using the stock while hot, skim fat (step 1). Or, chill stock and lift off fat with a fork (step 2). Makes about 8 cups.

Brown Sauce

In heavy saucepan melt 2 tablespoons *butter or margarine*. Blend in 2 tablespoons *all-purpose flour*. Cook and stir over medium-low heat for 15 to 20 minutes or till browned. Add 1½ cups *Beef Stock*. Bring to boiling, stirring constantly. Boil for 3 to 5 minutes. Reduce heat and simmer about 30 minutes or till reduced to 1 cup; stir frequently. Sauce should be slightly thinner than gravy. Serve with meat. Makes 1 cup.

Sauce Diable

In saucepan combine ¼ cup sliced *green onion*; 3 tablespoons *dry white wine*; and 8 to 10 whole *black peppercorns*, crushed. Boil 1 minute to reduce liquid. Add ½ cup *Brown Sauce*, 1 teaspoon snipped *parsley*, and ½ teaspoon *worcestershire sauce*; heat through. Serve with broiled steak. Makes about ⅔ cup.

1 If using the stock while hot, skim off fat. To skim, use a metal spoon to remove the oily liquid (fat) that rises to the top. A bulb baster also may be used to remove fat.

2 If stock is not used immediately, transfer it to straight-sided jars; cover and chill. The fat will solidify atop the stock during chilling. Lift off the fat layer with a fork.

Poultry

Tantalizing is the only word for the elegant poultry variations you'll find in this section. *Stuffed Chicken Rolls* rest atop a sherry-grape sauce (see recipe, page 23). A spicy yogurt marinade flavors *Tandoori Chicken* (see recipe, page 22). *Chicken Liver Pâté* can be baked and served in a terrine (see recipe, page 26), and delicately flavored *Chicken in Aspic* is shown garnished with a bed of aspic cubes (see recipe, page 27).

Tandoori Chicken
(Tan-DOOR-e Chicken)

In India, this chicken is cooked in a jar-shaped clay oven, called a tandoor. This distinctive main dish is pictured on pages 20 and 21—

- 2 2½- to 3-pound broiler-fryer chickens
- 2 tablespoons lemon juice
- 1½ teaspoons salt
- 2 tablespoons boiling water
- 1 teaspoon thread saffron, crushed
- 1 cup plain yogurt
- 3 cloves garlic, minced
- 2 tablespoons finely chopped gingerroot
- 2 teaspoons ground cumin
- 2 teaspoons ground coriander
- 1 teaspoon paprika
- ½ teaspoon cayenne
- ½ teaspoon red food coloring (optional)
- 2 tablespoons butter *or* margarine, melted
  Green pepper rings (optional)
  Onion rings (optional)

Skin chickens. Pat cavities and outside surfaces dry with paper toweling. Cut deep slits in chickens (step 1). Combine lemon juice and salt; rub over chickens, pressing mixture into slits.

In small bowl pour boiling water over crushed saffron; let stand for 10 minutes. For marinade, combine yogurt, garlic, gingerroot, cumin, coriander, paprika, cayenne, and food coloring; mix well. Place each chicken in a mixing bowl. Drizzle *half* of the saffron water over each chicken. Rub *half* of the marinade over each chicken (step 2). Cover and marinate chickens in the refrigerator for 24 hours.

Place chickens on rack in shallow roasting pan. Brush with melted butter or margarine. Roast, uncovered, in 400° oven for 15 minutes. Reduce temperature to 350°; roast about 1 hour more or till tender. Garnish with green pepper rings and onion rings, if desired. Makes 8 servings.

1 Cut deep slits in the skinned chickens with a sharp knife, as shown. Make several cuts in the thighs, drumsticks, breasts, and wings.

2 Rub the yogurt marinade over the entire surface of the chicken with your hands, as shown. Press the marinade into the deep slits to allow the flavors to penetrate into the meat.

Menu Suggestion

Complement the spicy entrée with these flavor-pleasing selections. Hot chutney is a traditional Indian accompaniment.

Tandoori Chicken
Warm pita bread rounds
Butter   Chutney
Vegetable Vinaigrette
(see recipe, page 58)

Coffee Custard
(see recipe, page 79)

Stuffed Chicken Rolls

For an elegant presentation, pour the sauce onto a platter and arrange chicken rolls atop. Garnish with cooked julienne strips of carrot and celery, serve with additional julienne vegetables. Pictured on pages 20 and 21—

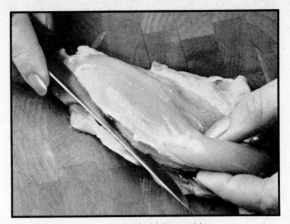

1 Hold chicken breast half with bone side down, as shown. Starting from the breastbone side, use a sharp knife to begin cutting the meat away from the bone. Cut as close to the bone as possible.

- 3 **whole large chicken breasts**
- 2 **cups soft bread cubes**
- 1½ **cups seedless green grapes, halved**
- ¼ **cup sliced almonds**
- ¼ **teaspoon ground coriander**
- ¼ **cup butter *or* margarine, melted**
- 1 **beaten egg**
- ¼ **cup all-purpose flour**
- ½ **cup fine dry bread crumbs**
- ¼ **cup butter *or* margarine**
- 2 **tablespoons butter *or* margarine**
- ¼ **cup light *or* dark raisins**
- 2 **teaspoons sugar**
- ⅛ **teaspoon ground allspice**
- ½ **cup Chicken Stock (see recipe, page 29)**
- ¼ **cup dry sherry**
- 1 **tablespoon cornstarch**

Halve chicken breasts lengthwise; skin. Remove and discard bones from chicken (steps 1 and 2). Place each piece of chicken between two pieces of clear plastic wrap. Pound out from center with meat mallet into a 5½x5½-inch square. Remove wrap. For stuffing, combine soft bread cubes, ½ *cup* grapes, almonds, and coriander; toss with ¼ cup melted butter.

Spoon about ¼ *cup* of the stuffing onto *each* piece of chicken. Fold in sides; roll up jelly-roll style (step 3). Skewer closed with wooden picks. Combine egg and 1 tablespoon *water*. Roll chicken in flour, then dip in egg mixture. Roll in dry bread crumbs. Cover and chill at least 1 hour. In skillet brown cold chicken rolls on all sides in ¼ cup butter. Transfer to 10x6x2-inch baking dish. Bake in 350° oven about 30 minutes or till chicken is tender.

Meanwhile, for sauce melt 2 tablespoons butter; stir in raisins, sugar, and allspice. Stir in Chicken Stock and sherry. Combine cornstarch and 2 tablespoons *cold water*; add to sherry mixture. Cook and stir till thickened and bubbly. Add remaining 1 cup grapes; cook for 1 to 2 minutes more. Remove wooden picks from chicken; serve chicken with sauce. Serves 6.

2 Continue cutting the meat from the bone. Use a sawing motion, pressing the flat side of the knife blade against the rib bones. With the other hand, gently pull the meat away from the rib bones.

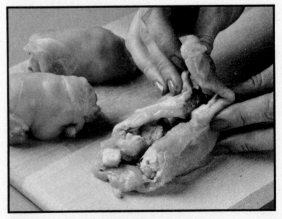

3 Spoon about ¼ cup stuffing onto each piece of chicken. Fold in the sides. Roll up chicken jelly-roll style, as shown. Make sure the folded sides are inside the roll. Fasten securely.

Coq au Vin
(Coke o VAWN)

2 ounces bacon (4 slices) *or* diced salt
    pork
1 2½- to 3-pound broiler-fryer chicken,
    cut up
½ teaspoon salt
⅛ teaspoon pepper
2 tablespoons cognac *or* other brandy
1 tablespoon all-purpose flour
1 cup burgundy
1 clove garlic, halved
1 bay leaf
¼ teaspoon dried rosemary
¼ teaspoon dried thyme
8 ounces boiling onions (about 8 onions)
1 cup whole fresh mushrooms
½ cup thinly sliced carrot
1 stalk celery, chopped (about ½ cup)
2 tablespoons all-purpose flour
2 tablespoons butter *or* margarine,
    softened
  Snipped parsley

1 *Cut a small square from several thicknesses of cheesecloth; place garlic, bay leaf, and dried herbs in center. Bring edges together to form a bag. Tie with string.*
A bouquet garni is easily removed because the herbs are bundled up.

In a 12-inch skillet cook bacon or salt pork till crisp; remove from pan, reserving drippings. Crumble bacon. Add chicken pieces to skillet; sprinkle with the salt and pepper. Brown chicken over medium heat about 15 minutes, turning to brown evenly. Pour cognac over chicken; carefully ignite. After flame subsides, remove chicken; set aside.

Stir 1 tablespoon flour into pan drippings. Add burgundy; cook and stir till bubbly. Tie garlic, bay leaf, rosemary, and thyme in cheesecloth to make a *bouquet garni* (step 1); add to skillet. Return chicken to skillet; add bacon or salt pork, onions, mushrooms, carrot, and celery. Bring to boiling; reduce heat. Cover and simmer about 35 minutes or till chicken and vegetables are tender. Remove chicken and vegetables from wine mixture; arrange in serving dish. Keep warm. Discard the *bouquet garni*.

Blend the 2 tablespoons flour and the softened butter or margarine into a smooth paste. Stir paste into hot mixture in skillet (step 2). Cook and stir till thickened and bubbly. Season to taste with salt and pepper. To serve, pour wine mixture over chicken and vegetables. Sprinkle with parsley. Makes 4 servings.

2 *Stir the flour-butter paste into the hot wine mixture in the skillet, as shown. Use a small wire whisk or wooden spoon to blend the paste in smoothly.*

Menu Suggestion

Plan a simple yet elegant meal around this well-seasoned French chicken dish.

Coq au Vin
Parslied potatoes
Buttered green peas
Mixed salad greens
Almond Torte
(see recipe, page 84)

24

Chicken in Aspic

These individually molded aspics make striking entrées for a luncheon or a light meal. Pictured on pages 20 and 21—

- 2 whole chicken breasts
- 4 cups water
- 1 cup dry white wine
- 3 stalks celery with leaves, chopped
- 1 small onion, quartered
- 1 bay leaf
- 1½ teaspoons salt
- ¼ teaspoon dried savory, crushed
- ¼ teaspoon dried rosemary, crushed
- 1 egg white
- 1 eggshell, crushed
- 2 envelopes unflavored gelatin
- 1 avocado
- ½ cup sliced pitted ripe olives

Place chicken breasts in large saucepan. Add water, wine, celery, onion, bay leaf, salt, savory, and rosemary. Bring to boiling; reduce heat. Cover and simmer about 20 minutes or till chicken is tender. Remove chicken and cool. Discard skin and bones. Cube chicken; set aside. Strain cooking liquid; discard vegetables. Skim fat from liquid; reserve 3¼ cups liquid.

Stir together egg white, eggshell, and ¼ cup *cold water*. Add to reserved 3¼ cups liquid; bring to boiling. Remove from heat; let stand for 5 minutes. Strain again through a sieve lined with several thicknesses of cheesecloth. Cool. Soften gelatin in strained liquid for 5 minutes. Heat and stir over low heat till gelatin is dissolved; remove from heat.

Using six individual 1-cup molds or 10-ounce custard cups (custard cups will not be completely filled), pour *3 tablespoons* gelatin mixture into *each* mold. Chill till slightly firm. Seed, peel, and slice avocado; halve slices. Using *half* the chicken and *half* the avocado, arrange atop gelatin. Arrange olives around edges (step 1). Spoon about *3 tablespoons* gelatin mixture into *each* mold. Chill till slightly firm. Arrange remaining chicken and avocado atop. Spoon remaining gelatin mixture into molds (step 2). (Or, arrange chicken, avocado, and olives in separate layers for a formal appearance.) Chill till firm. To serve, line serving plate with spinach leaves, if desired. Unmold aspics onto plate. Makes 6 servings.

1 Place chicken cubes and avocado pieces atop the slightly firm gelatin mixture, as shown. Position sliced olives around the edge. Arrange the foods in an even layer so the next layer of gelatin covers them uniformly.

2 Spoon the remaining gelatin mixture over the final layer of chicken and avocado. Cover the ingredients completely with the gelatin.

Aspic Garnish

To use aspic for garnishing, trim serving plate with small cubes of the clear gel.

Prepare Chicken in Aspic as directed *except* prepare gelatin mixture reserving 3¾ *cups* of the wine liquid. Pour ½ cup of the gelatin mixture into an 8x4x2-inch loaf pan. Chill till firm. With a knife or a fork, cut gel in loaf pan into ¼-inch cubes. Spoon around molded aspics.

Orange Pheasant

Cooking in a covered clay pot is becoming more and more popular. You don't have to add fat and the food stays juicy—

- **2 2- to 3-pound pheasants** *or* **whole roasting chickens**
- **1½ teaspoons fresh sage** *or* **½ teaspoon dried sage, crushed**
- **½ teaspoon salt**
- **2 teaspoons finely shredded orange peel**
- **2 oranges, peeled and chopped**
- **½ cup orange juice**
- **½ cup dry white wine**
- **2 tablespoons brown sugar**
- **2 tablespoons cider vinegar**
- **2 whole cloves**
- **¼ teaspoon ground ginger**
- **4 teaspoons cornstarch**
- **1 tablespoon orange liqueur**

Use a partially glazed or unglazed clay pot*. To prepare clay pot, fill the pot and the upturned lid with water. Let stand about 10 minutes, then drain water from pot and lid.

Sprinkle cavities of birds with sage, salt, and ¼ teaspoon *pepper*. Fill body cavities with chopped orange (step 1). Tie legs together and bind wings to body; tie bird into a compact shape (step 2). Place birds, breast side up, in clay pot (step 3). Combine orange juice, wine, brown sugar, vinegar, cloves, and ginger; pour over pheasants. Cover pot and place in a cold oven; set temperature at 400°. Bake for 1¼ hours. Remove lid; bake about 10 minutes more. (Very heavy or thick pots may require more baking time.) Remove clay pot from oven and place on a trivet or potholder (do not place on a cold surface). Transfer birds to warm serving platter; remove string and discard chopped orange. Keep birds warm.

For sauce, pour pan juices into liquid measure; skim off fat. Strain juices; reserve 1½ cups of the liquid. In small saucepan combine cornstarch and orange liqueur. Add reserved 1½ cups liquid and orange peel. Cook and stir till thickened and bubbly. Spoon some sauce over birds; pass remainder. Garnish with orange slices and watercress, if desired. Serves 4 to 6.

Or, use a covered roasting pan instead of a clay pot. Bake birds about 1½ hours (total time).

1 Place pheasant, neck end down, in a mixing bowl. Spoon chopped orange into body cavity of pheasant. Repeat with the remaining pheasant.

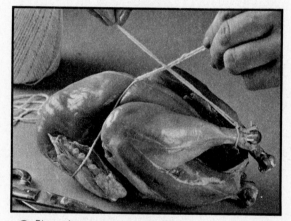

2 Place pheasant on its back. Tie the legs together with string. Tie a second piece of string around bird to bind the wings to the body. Connect the two strings with a third piece of string, as shown, and tie bird into a compact shape.

3 Position pheasants, side by side, in clay pot. Place the birds breast side up. Combine orange juice, wine, brown sugar, vinegar, and spices in a 2-cup liquid measure. Pour over pheasants in clay pot.

Chicken Stock

**Bony chicken pieces (backs, necks, and
      wings) from 2 chickens**
- 2 **cups sliced leeks**
- 3 **stalks celery with leaves, chopped**
- 1 **carrot, quartered**
- 2 **bay leaves**
- 1½ **teaspoons salt**
- 1 **teaspoon whole black peppercorns,
     cracked**
- 3 **whole cloves**

In Dutch oven combine all ingredients and 6
cups *water*. Bring to boiling. Reduce heat; cover
and simmer for 1 hour or till meat is tender.
Remove chicken; strain stock. Discard chicken
and vegetables. If using stock while hot, skim
fat. Or, chill stock and lift off fat. (See Beef
Stock, page 19, steps 1 and 2.) Makes 5 cups.

Chicken Consommé

To clarify stock, stir together ¼ cup cold *water*;
1 *egg white*; and 1 *eggshell*, crushed. Add to
strained *Chicken Stock*; bring to boiling.
Remove from heat and let stand 5 minutes.
Strain again through a cheesecloth-lined sieve
(step 1).

Madrilene Consommé

Sprinkle 1 envelope *unflavored gelatin* over ½
cup *tomato juice*; stir into 1½ cups boiling
Chicken Consommé. Stir to dissolve; remove
from heat. Turn mixture into a bowl. Add
another ½ cup *tomato juice*, 3 tablespoons *dry
sherry*, and dash *white pepper*. Chill till partially
set by placing bowl into a larger bowl of ice
water; stir occasionally (step 2). Chill till almost
firm. Spoon into dishes and garnish with snipped chives to serve as a first-course soup.
Makes 4 servings.

1 To strain the stock, line a sieve
with 1 or 2 layers of cheesecloth;
set over a large bowl. Pour stock
mixture through. Discard the cooked
egg and any other small particles. The
clarified stock is called consommé.

2 Place the bowl of gelatin mixture
into a larger bowl of ice water. Chill
gelatin mixture till partially set, stirring
occasionally. The consistency of the
gelatin at this stage is similar to that of
unbeaten egg whites, as shown. Once
the mixture is partially set, remove bowl
of ice water and chill gelatin mixture in
refrigerator till almost firm.

Stock Substitutes

When Chicken Stock or Beef Stock is
called for in a recipe, use the stock recipes
in this book (see Beef Stock, page 19) or
one of the excellent alternatives available.
Consider canned chicken or beef broth
used straight from the can or *condensed*
chicken or beef broth, which must be di-
luted according to can directions. Instant
chicken- or beef-flavored bouillon
granules dissolved in water work fine, too.

Fish & Seafood

The versatility of fish and seafood is evident in this section, where it's prepared simple or fancy, as appetizer or main dish. A Mexican food, *Ceviche* is raw fish marinated and "cooked" in lime or lemon juice (see recipe, page 36). Tempting *Lobster Thermidor* makes an elegant dinner for two (see recipe, page 37). And rich-tasting *Salmon Mousse*, prepared in a fancy fish mold, is easy to serve at a buffet with crisp crackers (see recipe, page 38).

Oysters Rockefeller

You may decide to substitute drained, shucked oysters and small baking shells for fresh oysters in shells—

24 oysters in shells
1 cup finely chopped cooked spinach
¼ cup fine dry bread crumbs
2 tablespoons finely chopped celery
2 tablespoons snipped parsley
1 tablespoon finely chopped green onion
¾ teaspoon salt
½ teaspoon pepper
¼ teaspoon dried basil, crushed
¼ teaspoon paprika
¾ cup butter *or* margarine, softened
¼ cup fine dry bread crumbs
1 tablespoon butter *or* margarine, melted
Rock salt

Refer to Fried Clams, page 39 (steps 1 and 2). Thoroughly rinse oysters in cold water. Hold the oyster shell firmly on a flat surface with flat side up. Insert an oyster knife or other blunt-tipped knife between the shell halves. Cut around the opening close to the flat upper shell and pry off the top shell. Loosen and remove the oyster from the bottom shell with knife. Remove any bits of shell that may cling to the oyster. Discard the flat upper shells; wash the deep bottom shells. Place each oyster in bottom half of shell.

In mixing bowl combine spinach, ¼ cup bread crumbs, celery, parsley, green onion, salt, pepper, basil, and paprika. Add ¾ cup softened butter or margarine. Beat till mixture is well blended (step 1). Toss together ¼ cup bread crumbs and 1 tablespoon melted butter.

Arrange oyster shells on a bed of rock salt in shallow baking pan. Spoon about *1 tablespoon* of the spinach mixture atop *each* oyster (step 2). Sprinkle with buttered bread crumbs. Bake in 450° oven about 10 minutes or till crumb mixture is lightly browned and edges of oysters begin to curl. Makes 6 to 8 appetizer servings.

1 Beat together the spinach mixture and the softened butter or margarine with a wooden spoon till well mixed. Since the ingredients are not smooth, the mixture will appear lumpy, as shown.

2 Arrange oyster shells on a bed of rock salt in baking pan to prevent them from tipping. Drop spinach mixture from a tablespoon onto each oyster. Use a spatula to push mixture off spoon.

4 **fresh** *or* **frozen sole fillets (about 1 pound)**
¼ **cup finely chopped celery**
3 **tablespoons finely chopped onion**
2 **tablespoons butter** *or* **margarine**
1 **cup dry bread cubes**
1 **small orange**
1 **tablespoon snipped parsley**
¼ **teaspoon salt**
   Dash pepper
3 **tablespoons butter** *or* **margarine, melted**
   Snipped parsley
   Orange slices

Thaw fish, if frozen. Sprinkle fillets with a little salt and pepper. For filling, cook celery and onion in 2 tablespoons butter or margarine till tender. Remove from heat; toss with bread cubes. Finely shred enough peel from orange to measure *1 teaspoon*. Peel and section orange; chop orange sections. Add chopped orange, orange peel, 1 tablespoon parsley, salt, and pepper to bread cube mixture; mix well.

Spoon about ¼ *cup* of the filling atop *each* fillet. Wrap fish around filling and secure with wooden picks (step 1). Arrange stuffed fillets in a greased 9x9x2-inch baking pan. Brush with *2 tablespoons* of the melted butter or margarine. Bake, uncovered, in 350° oven about 20 minutes or till fish flakes easily when tested with a fork (step 2). Brush with the remaining melted butter or margarine and sprinkle with additional snipped parsley before serving. Garnish with orange slices. Makes 4 servings.

Lemon-Stuffed Fillets

Use ingredients listed above *except* add ¼ teaspoon *curry powder*, ½ teaspoon finely shredded *lemon peel*, and 4 teaspoons *lemon juice*; increase dry bread cubes to 1¼ *cups*, and omit chopped orange sections and orange peel. Prepare fish fillets as above. For filling, cook celery and onion with curry powder in 2 tablespoons butter till tender. Remove from heat. Toss with bread cubes. Add lemon peel, lemon juice, 1 tablespoon parsley, salt, and pepper to bread cube mixture; mix well. Continue stuffing and baking fillets as above. Garnish with *lemon slices* instead of orange slices.

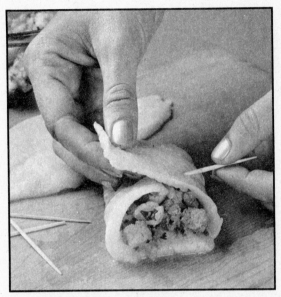

1 To stuff fish fillets, lay fish flat on cutting board. Place filling in center of the fillet. Bring ends of fish together and overlap atop filling. Secure with wooden picks.

2 When fish is done, it will become opaque, white, and tender. To test for doneness, insert a fork at a 45-degree angle and twist the fork gently. Fish should flake easily, as shown.

Creamy Sauced Shrimp

Court Bouillon is a seasoned broth traditionally used to poach or boil seafood. When preparing this sauced shrimp recipe, cook the shrimp in the Court Bouillon for added flavor, or simply use the water and salt from the bouillon recipe—

Court Bouillon
- 1½ pounds fresh *or* frozen shrimp in shells
- 1 cup sliced fresh mushrooms
- ½ cup sliced green onion
- ¼ cup finely chopped green pepper
- 5 tablespoons butter *or* margarine
- 2 tablespoons all-purpose flour
- 1 tablespoon snipped parsley
- 1 tablespoon chopped pimiento
- ½ teaspoon salt
- ½ teaspoon dry mustard
- ¼ teaspoon pepper
- 2 tablespoons dry white wine
- 1 tablespoon all-purpose flour
- 1 cup dairy sour cream
- Patty Shells* (see recipe, page 80) *or* hot cooked rice

Bring Court Bouillon to boiling. Add fresh or frozen shrimp. Return to boiling; reduce heat. Cover and simmer for 1 to 3 minutes or till shrimp turn pink. Remove shrimp with slotted spoon; set aside. Strain Court Bouillon; discard solids. Return Court Bouillon to saucepan; bring to boiling. Boil, uncovered, about 15 minutes or till liquid is reduced to 1½ cups; set aside.

Meanwhile, peel shrimp, removing tails (step 1). With a sharp knife, make a shallow slit along the back of the shrimp; remove the sandy black vein (step 2). If shrimp are large, halve lengthwise. Set shrimp aside.

In a 10-inch skillet cook mushrooms, green onion, and green pepper in *3 tablespoons* of the butter or margarine till tender. Remove vegetables and set aside. Melt the remaining butter or margarine in skillet; stir in 2 tablespoons flour. Add the reduced 1½ cups Court Bouillon liquid. Cook and stir till thickened and bubbly. Stir in mushroom mixture, parsley, pimiento, salt, dry mustard, and pepper. Stir in shrimp and wine; heat through. Blend 1 tablespoon flour into sour cream; stir into shrimp mixture. Heat through; *do not boil*. Serve in Patty Shells* or over hot cooked rice. Makes 6 servings.

*If desired, substitute frozen patty shells, baked, for the homemade shells.

Court Bouillon: In large saucepan combine 5 cups *water*; 2 stalks *celery*, chopped; 1 small *onion*, chopped; 2 *lemon slices*; 2 *bay leaves*; 1 sprig *parsley*; and 1 teaspoon *salt*. Bring to boiling; cover and simmer for 30 minutes.

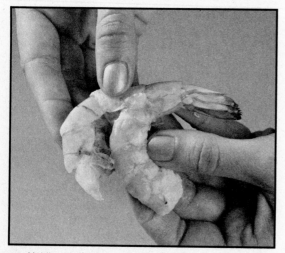

1 Holding shrimp in one hand, carefully peel back the shell, as shown. Remove the last section of the shell and the tail. Repeat with remaining shrimp.

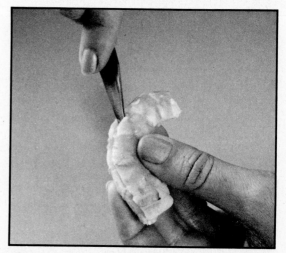

2 With a sharp knife, make a shallow slit along the back of the shrimp; look for a sandy black vein. If present, use the knife tip to scrape out the vein.

Coquilles Saint Jacques

(Co-KEY Sawn Zshawk)

1½ pounds fresh *or* frozen scallops
1 cup dry white wine
1 tablespoon lemon juice
2 sprigs parsley
1 bay leaf
½ teaspoon salt
1 cup chopped fresh mushrooms
2 tablespoons thinly sliced shallot *or* green onion
2 tablespoons butter *or* margarine
2 tablespoons all-purpose flour
¼ teaspoon salt
⅛ teaspoon ground nutmeg
    Dash pepper
½ cup milk
2 egg yolks
½ cup light cream
1 cup soft bread crumbs
2 tablespoons butter *or* margarine, melted

Thaw scallops, if frozen. Halve any large scallops. In saucepan combine scallops, wine, lemon juice, parsley, bay leaf, and ½ teaspoon salt. Bring to boiling; reduce heat. Cover and simmer for 2 to 4 minutes or till scallops are opaque in appearance. Remove scallops with a slotted spoon. Strain wine mixture through cheesecloth; reserve 1 cup liquid (step 1).

In skillet cook mushrooms and shallot or green onion in 2 tablespoons butter or margarine about 5 minutes or till tender. Stir in flour, ¼ teaspoon salt, nutmeg, and pepper. Add reserved 1 cup liquid and milk. Cook and stir till thickened and bubbly. Remove from heat. Combine egg yolks and cream; beat well with a wire whisk. Gradually stir about *half* of the hot mixture into egg yolk mixture; return to remaining hot mixture in skillet. Add scallops. Heat and stir just till bubbly. Reduce heat; cook and stir over low heat for 2 minutes.

Place 6 buttered coquilles (baking shells), shallow individual casseroles, or 6-ounce custard cups in shallow baking pans. Spoon scallop mixture into shells (step 2). Toss together bread crumbs and 2 tablespoons melted butter or margarine; sprinkle over scallop mixture. Bake in 400° oven about 10 minutes or till browned. Makes 6 servings.

1 Strain seasonings from wine mixture. To strain, line a sieve with one or two layers of cheesecloth; set over a 2-cup liquid measure. Pour the wine mixture through the sieve. Reserve 1 cup of the liquid; discard the seasonings.

2 Place coquilles (baking shells), casseroles, or custard cups in shallow baking pans. Spoon about ½ cup of the scallop mixture into each shell. You can buy coquilles in kitchen shops or in kitchen departments of larger stores.

Menu Suggestion

The French entrée features scallops in a creamy wine sauce baked in the shell. We've selected accompaniments that don't overwhelm the seafood flavor.

Coquilles Saint Jacques
Stuffed Artichokes
(see recipe, page 54)

Hard rolls   Butter
Fresh fruit with orange liqueur

Ceviche
(Suh-VEESH)

Also known as seviche, this delicate dish gets its characteristic flavor and texture from the lime or lemon juice that "cooks" the fish. Pictured on pages 30 and 31—

- **1 pound fresh *or* frozen haddock fillets *or* other fish fillets**
- **1 cup lime juice *or* lemon juice**
- **1 small onion**
- **2 or 3 pickled Serrano *or* jalapeño peppers**
- **¼ cup olive oil *or* cooking oil**
- **¼ teaspoon dried oregano, crushed**
- **2 medium tomatoes**

Thaw fish, if frozen. Cut fish into ½-inch cubes. In a nonmetal bowl, cover fish with lime or lemon juice. Cover and chill 4 hours or overnight till fish is opaque; stir occasionally (step 1).

Thinly slice onion; separate into rings. Rinse, seed, and cut Serrano peppers into strips (step 2). Add onion, peppers, olive oil or cooking oil, oregano, ¾ teaspoon *salt*, and ⅛ teaspoon *pepper* to fish. Toss gently till well combined; cover and chill. Peel, seed, and chop tomatoes; toss with chilled fish mixture. Turn into serving bowl. Garnish with pepper flower, if desired. Makes 10 to 12 appetizer servings.

1 Place cubed fish fillets in a nonmetal bowl and cover with fresh lime juice or lemon juice. Cover and refrigerate for at least 4 hours or overnight, stirring occasionally. The fish will become opaque as the acid in the juice "cooks" the fish.

2 Rinse the Serrano peppers in cold running water and cut open. Hold the pepper with a fork, as shown, and use a knife to scrape out the seeds and fleshy veins. Slice the peppers into strips.

Ways to Serve Caviar

When an occasion calls for special fare, reach for a jar of caviar (fish eggs or roe). You can choose black caviar from sturgeon (the most expensive), herring, whitefish, or lumpfish; or red caviar from salmon, cod, or tuna.

This delicacy is usually served as an appetizer. Set a bowl of caviar in crushed ice; serve with thin slices of melba or fresh toast and a selection of accompaniments such as lemon wedges, sieved hard-cooked egg yolk, minced onion, or snipped chives. You also can fold caviar into dips, spreads, or stuffed egg fillings. Be sure to reserve a little for a garnish.

Lobster Thermidor

If desired, garnish this stylish entrée for two with lemon wedges dipped in snipped parsley. Pictured on pages 30 and 31—

- **2 1- to 1½-pound live lobsters**
- **1 cup sliced fresh mushrooms**
- **4 shallots, chopped**
- **4 tablespoons butter *or* margarine**
- **4 teaspoons all-purpose flour**
- **½ cup light cream**
- **¼ cup dry sherry**
- **½ teaspoon dry mustard**
- **¼ teaspoon paprika**
- **2 egg yolks**
- **½ cup butter *or* margarine, melted**
- **1 tablespoon lemon juice**

In large kettle bring 12 cups *water* and 1 tablespoon *salt* to boiling. Holding one lobster firmly just behind the eyes, rinse it in cold running water. Plunge lobster headfirst into boiling salted water. Repeat with other lobster. Return to boiling; reduce heat and simmer for 20 minutes. Remove lobsters at once. Cut lobster in half lengthwise (step 1). Remove black vein and body organs; reserve red coral roe and brownish-green liver (step 2). Crack open large claws (step 3). Break claws away from body. Remove and reserve meat from claws, tail, and body. Cut meat into chunks. Clean and reserve shells, keeping them intact.

Cook mushrooms and shallot in *2 tablespoons* of the butter till tender. Stir in lobster meat, liver, and roe. In another saucepan melt additional 2 tablespoons butter. Stir in flour; add cream. Cook and stir till bubbly. Stir in sherry, mustard, paprika, ¼ teaspoon *salt*, and dash white *pepper*. Stir in lobster mixture; keep hot.

For sauce, in heat-proof bowl combine egg yolks, 1 tablespoon *water*, and dash *salt*. Place bowl over a saucepan of boiling water to serve as a double boiler. Using a wire whisk, whip briskly till warm and creamy. Remove from heat. Beat in ½ cup melted butter, adding it very slowly at the beginning. Stir in lemon juice. Return to heat; cook and stir till blended. Place lobster shells in broiler pan. Spoon hot lobster mixture into shells; spoon sauce atop. Immediately broil 6 inches from heat about 2 minutes or till hot. Serves 2.

1 Place each lobster on its back. With sharp knife and scissors, cut lobster completely in half lengthwise, cutting through shell back and tail section.

2 Using the tip of a sharp knife, scrape out the black vein that runs the length of the lobster, if present. Remove and discard all the organs that are in the body cavity near the head. Remove and reserve the roe (found only in females) and the liver.

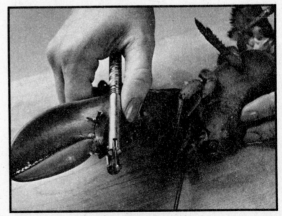

3 Use a nutcracker or lobster cracker to crack open large claws of the lobster. Break claws away from the body; remove lobster meat to use in filling.

"Mousse" is French for "foam." This creamy, delicate salmon spread is pictured on pages 30 and 31 —

- 1   15½-ounce can red salmon
- 2   envelopes unflavored gelatin
- 1   teaspoon sugar
- 1¼ cups mayonnaise *or* salad dressing
- ¼   cup tomato sauce
- 2   tablespoons lemon juice
- 2   teaspoons worcestershire sauce
- ½   cup finely chopped celery
- 2   hard-cooked eggs, chopped
- 2   tablespoons snipped chives
- ¼   teaspoon pepper
- ½   cup whipping cream
-     Lettuce (optional)
-     Thin cucumber slices
-     Fresh dill
-     Assorted crackers

Drain salmon, reserving the liquid; add water, if necessary, to equal 1 cup liquid. Bone and flake salmon; set aside. In a small saucepan sprinkle unflavored gelatin and sugar over the reserved 1 cup salmon liquid. Heat, stirring constantly, till gelatin dissolves. Remove from heat.

Combine mayonnaise or salad dressing, tomato sauce, lemon juice, and worcestershire sauce; stir in gelatin mixture. Chill till partially set (step 1). Fold in salmon, celery, chopped hard-cooked eggs, chives, and pepper.

Beat whipping cream till soft peaks form. Fold whipped cream into gelatin mixture (step 2). Pour into a 6-cup fish-shaped mold or ring mold. Chill till firm. To serve, line a tray or serving plate with lettuce, if desired. Unmold mousse onto tray. Garnish with cucumber slices and fresh dill. Serve with assorted crackers. Makes 8 servings.

1 *Gelatin is partially set when it has a consistency similar to unbeaten egg whites, as shown. Solid ingredients can be folded in at this stage and remain evenly distributed throughout the mixture.*

2 *To fold in whipped cream, cut down through mixture with a rubber spatula. Scrape across bottom of bowl; then bring spatula up and over mixture, close to the surface. Repeat circular down-up-and-over motion till mixture is completely folded together, turning the bowl as you work.*

Menu Suggestion

Give Salmon Mousse a center spot on your appetizer table. An assortment of hot and cold tidbits completes the party menu.

Salmon Mousse

Cocktail meatballs

Assorted dips   Vegetable dippers

Cheese tray   Crackers

Creamy Stuffed Eggs

(see recipe, page 47)

Fried Clams

24 fresh *or* frozen clams in shells
⅓ cup all-purpose flour
⅛ teaspoon cayenne
2 beaten eggs
2 tablespoons lemon juice
½ cup finely crushed crackers
¼ cup grated parmesan cheese
Cooking oil *or* shortening for deep-fat frying
Cocktail Sauce (optional)

Thaw clams, if frozen. Thoroughly rinse clams in cold water. Hold the clam in one hand and insert knife blade between shell halves (step 1). Cut around the opening. Twist the knife up to pry shell open (step 2). Pull up top half of shell. Cut the muscle free from top and bottom halves of shell. Pat clams dry with paper toweling.

In shallow bowl stir together flour and cayenne. In another bowl combine beaten eggs and lemon juice. In shallow bowl combine crushed crackers and parmesan cheese. Roll clams in seasoned flour, then dip flour-coated clams in egg mixture, letting excess drip off. Roll in crushed cracker mixture. (Coat only enough clams to fry at one time, and fry immediately after coating.)

In saucepan or deep-fat fryer, heat cooking oil or shortening to 375°. Fry a few clams at a time in hot fat about 1 minute or till golden. Remove with slotted spoon; drain on paper toweling (step 3). Keep Fried Clams hot in a 325° oven while frying the remaining clams. Serve Fried Clams with Cocktail Sauce if desired, spearing the clams with cocktail picks. Makes 24 appetizers.

Cocktail Sauce: In saucepan cook 1 tablespoon finely chopped *green pepper*, 1 teaspoon *grated onion*, and 1 small clove *garlic*, minced, in 1 tablespoon *butter or margarine* till green pepper is tender. Stir in 3 medium *tomatoes*, peeled, quartered, and seeded; 1 tablespoon prepared *horseradish*; 2 teaspoons *lemon juice*; 2 teaspoons *worcestershire sauce*; ½ teaspoon *salt*; ¼ teaspoon *cayenne*; and ¼ teaspoon *chili powder*. Cover and cook over low heat for 5 minutes. Uncover; continue cooking about 10 minutes longer. Force tomato mixture through a fine sieve. Serve warm or chilled.

1 To shuck or open clams, hold the clam in one hand with the hinged side of the clam against the palm, as shown. Insert a knife blade between the top and bottom halves of the shell.

2 Hold the shell firmly and cut around the opening. Twist the knife up slightly to pry the shell open. Pull up the top half of the shell with your thumb.

3 In a saucepan or deep-fat fryer, heat about 2 inches of oil or shortening to 375°. Carefully lower a few clams into hot fat. Cook about 1 minute or till golden. Remove from fat with a slotted spoon; drain well on paper toweling.

Pike Quenelles

(Pike Ca-NELL)

Serve these elegant dumplings for a first course or as a dinner accompaniment —

1 **pound fresh** *or* **frozen skinless and boneless pike** *or* **cod fillets**
½ **cup water**
¼ **cup butter** *or* **margarine**
½ **cup all-purpose flour**
½ **teaspoon salt**
⅛ **teaspoon ground nutmeg**
   Dash pepper
2 **eggs**
2 **egg whites**
2 **tablespoons light cream**
3 **cups hot water**
¾ **teaspoon salt**
   Mornay Sauce (see recipe, page 41)
   Snipped parsley

Thaw fish, if frozen. In saucepan bring ½ cup water and butter or margarine to boiling, stirring till butter melts. Add flour, ½ teaspoon salt, nutmeg, and pepper all at once; stir vigorously till well blended. Cook and stir over low heat till mixture forms a ball that does not separate. Remove from heat. Cool for 10 minutes. Beat in eggs, then egg whites. Set mixture aside.

Pat fish dry with paper toweling. Chop fish. Process in blender or food processor container,

⅓ at a time. Stop frequently to scrape down sides. Beat fish and cream into flour mixture (step 1). Cover and chill thoroughly.

Grease a 12-inch skillet. Using two soup spoons, mold a scant 2 tablespoons fish mixture into an oval shape (step 2); gently place in skillet. (Or, for large quenelles mold a scant ¼ cup fish mixture into an oval shape.) Repeat with remaining fish mixture. Combine 3 cups hot water and ¾ teaspoon salt; gently pour down side of skillet. Bring just to simmering. Cover and simmer very gently about 10 minutes for the small quenelles and about 15 minutes for the large quenelles or till set. Remove from skillet with slotted spoon; drain on paper toweling (step 3). Serve immediately with Mornay Sauce. Garnish with snipped parsley. Makes 30 small or 12 to 14 large quenelles.

Pike Mousse

Prepare Pike Quenelles as above *except* increase light cream to ¼ *cup*. Turn fish mixture into 4 greased individual 1-cup baking dishes. Place in a 13x9x2-inch baking pan on oven rack. Pour hot water into pan around baking dishes to a depth of 1 inch. Bake in 350° oven about 30 minutes or till lightly browned. Serves 4.

1 Process the chopped fish in a blender or food processor. The mixture will appear lumpy. Add fish and cream to the flour mixture; beat with a wooden spoon till well blended.

2 Scoop out a scant 2 tablespoons of fish mixture with a soup spoon, mold the fish mixture into an oval shape; as shown. Gently place in greased skillet.

3 Cook the quenelles in gently simmering salted water till set. Carefully remove from skillet with a slotted spoon; drain well on paper toweling. Serve immediately.

Béchamel Sauce

This sauce, also known as white sauce, is the basis for many recipes—

- 2 **tablespoons butter** *or* **margarine**
- 2 **tablespoons all-purpose flour**
- ¼ **teaspoon salt**
- **Dash pepper**
- 1 **cup milk**

In small heavy saucepan melt butter or margarine. Blend in flour, salt, and pepper (step 1). Add milk all at once (step 2). Cook and stir over medium heat till thickened and bubbly. Cook and stir 2 minutes more. Makes 1 cup.

Lemon-Chive Sauce

Stir 1 tablespoon snipped *chives* and 2 teaspoons *lemon juice* into cooked Béchamel Sauce. Serve with boiled potatoes, cooked asparagus, or fish.

Herb-Garlic Sauce

Prepare Béchamel Sauce as above *except* cook 1 clove *garlic*, minced, in the butter or margarine before blending in flour, salt, and pepper. Continue as above. Stir ½ teaspoon dried *basil*, crushed, and ¼ teaspoon dried *tarragon*, crushed, into the cooked sauce. Serve with cooked carrots, broccoli, or green beans.

Cheese Sauce

Prepare Béchamel Sauce as above *except* increase milk to 1¼ cups. After cooking 2 minutes, stir in ½ cup shredded *American cheese* and ½ cup shredded *Swiss cheese*, stirring till melted. Serve over cooked vegetables.

Mornay Sauce

Melt 3 tablespoons *butter*; blend in 3 tablespoons all-purpose *flour*, ½ *teaspoon salt*, ⅛ teaspoon ground *nutmeg*, and dash *pepper*. Add 1¼ cups *light cream* all at once. Cook and stir till bubbly; cook and stir 2 minutes more. Stir in ¼ cup *dry white wine*. Add ⅓ cup shredded *Swiss cheese*; stir till melted. Serve with chicken, fish, or poached eggs. Makes 1¾ cups.

1 Blend the flour, salt, and pepper into the melted butter over low heat; stir till no lumps remain. This fat-flour mixture is often called a roux. The fat coats the flour particles to prevent lumps from forming when liquid is added.

2 With the saucepan over low heat, add the milk all at once. Stir constantly to evenly distribute the fat-flour mixture. The fat-flour mixture and the milk must be well blended to produce a creamy sauce free of lumps.

Eggs

Eggs can be prepared in so many ways that you'll want their gourmet touch at every meal. *Shrimp-Almond Quiche* makes a perfect appetizer or light entrée (see recipe, page 50), as does *French Omelet* with *Tarragon-Asparagus Filling* (see recipes, pages 48 and 49). Variations of appetizing *Liver-Stuffed Eggs* include *Creamy Stuffed Eggs*, *Stuffed Eggs Almondine*, and *Caviar-Stuffed Eggs* (see recipes, page 47). And for that elegant brunch, there's *Eggs Benedict* (see recipe, page 46).

Camembert Soufflé

Camembert cheese is a ripened, full-flavored, French cheese. Often served as an appetizer or dessert, it adds richness to this soufflé —

¼ cup finely chopped celery
2 tablespoons thinly sliced green onion
1 small clove garlic, minced
3 tablespoons butter *or* margarine
3 tablespoons all-purpose flour
1 teaspoon dry mustard
½ teaspoon salt
1 cup milk
5 ounces camembert cheese, rind removed and cubed, *or* shredded Swiss cheese
½ cup grated parmesan *or* romano cheese
5 egg yolks
7 egg whites

Place a buttered foil collar on a 2-quart soufflé dish, extending 2 inches above dish (step 1). Cook celery, onion, and garlic in butter till tender. Blend in flour, mustard, salt, and dash *pepper*. Add milk all at once; cook and stir till thickened and bubbly. Add camembert or Swiss cheese and parmesan or romano cheese, stirring to melt. Remove from heat; set aside.

Beat egg yolks 5 minutes or till thick and lemon-colored. Slowly add cheese mixture to egg yolks, stirring constantly. Wash beaters. Beat egg whites to stiff peaks; gradually pour the yolk mixture over beaten whites, folding to blend. Turn into prepared ungreased soufflé dish (step 2). For a "top hat" that puffs in the oven, use a spatula to trace a 1-inch-deep circle through the mixture about 1 inch from edge (step 3). Bake in 350° oven for 40 minutes or till a knife inserted near center comes out clean. Do not open oven door during baking. Test soufflé at the end of suggested baking time while soufflé is still in oven (step 4). Serve immediately, using 2 forks (step 5). Serves 6.

Camembert-Crab Soufflé

Prepare Camembert Soufflé as above *except* increase salt to ¾ *teaspoon* and omit parmesan cheese. Stir one 6-ounce can *crab meat*, drained, finely flaked, and cartilage removed, into cheese sauce. Continue as above.

1 Butter one side of a foil strip. To form a collar, place the foil strip around the soufflé dish with buttered side in, extending 2 inches above dish. Secure the foil strip with tape or a piece of string. After baking, remove collar.

2 Pour the egg-cheese mixture into the soufflé dish. Pour gently so that batter remains fluffy.

4 Bake in 350° oven for 40 minutes or till a knife inserted near center comes out clean. Test while soufflé is still in oven. When inserting knife, slightly enlarge hole by moving knife from side to side. Otherwise the crust may clean the knife as it is pulled out.

3 If you want the baked soufflé to have a "top hat," use a small flexible metal spatula to trace a 1-inch-deep circle through the mixture about 1 inch from the edge of the dish.

Menu Suggestion

This menu for a light lunch showcases the natural compatibility of fruit and cheese. Bake the Cream Puffs, then the soufflé.

Camembert Soufflé
Fruit salad
Breadsticks
Cream Puffs
(see recipe, page 83)

5 Serve soufflé immediately after removal from oven; otherwise, the soufflé may fall. To serve, insert two forks back to back and gently pull apart into individual servings. Use a spoon to transfer servings to plates.

Eggs Benedict

Pictured on pages 42 and 43—

6 slices Canadian-style bacon
6 eggs
   Hollandaise Sauce (see recipe, page 51)
6 rusks *or* 3 English muffins, split,
      toasted, and buttered
   Paprika (optional)

In a 12-inch skillet brown bacon over medium heat for 3 minutes on each side. Cover; keep warm. Lightly grease a 10-inch skillet. Add water to half-fill skillet; bring to boiling. Reduce heat; simmer. Break one egg into small dish; slide egg into water, holding lip of dish as close to water as possible. Repeat with remaining eggs so that each has equal amount of space (step 1). Simmer, uncovered, 3 to 5 minutes or till eggs are just soft-cooked. During cooking, smooth edges of eggs with a spoon (step 2). Remove with slotted spoon (step 3); place in large mixing bowl filled with warm water to keep eggs warm. Prepare Hollandaise Sauce.

   Top each rusk or English muffin half with a bacon slice and an egg; spoon on Hollandaise Sauce. Sprinkle with paprika, if desired. Serve immediately. Makes 6 servings.

Menu Suggestion

Breakfast or brunch is extra special when you serve Eggs Benedict. This menu uses fresh fruit to complement the richness of the Hollandaise Sauce.

Melon half with fresh strawberries
Eggs Benedict
Tomato juice

1 Carefully slide the egg into the water. Breaking the egg into a dish instead of directly into the water helps prevent breaking the yolk.

2 During cooking, smooth the edges of eggs by using a spoon to gently pull away any strings of trailing cooked egg white. For perfectly round eggs, place a metal egg ring in the simmering water. Slip egg into center of ring; remove ring as soon as the egg white sets.

3 When eggs are cooked to the desired doneness, lift out of water with slotted spoon. If desired, use kitchen shears to trim any remaining ragged edges.

Liver-Stuffed Eggs

Several filling variations are pictured on pages 42 and 43 —

- **8 eggs**
- **¼ pound chicken livers**
- **3 tablespoons mayonnaise *or* salad dressing**
- **1 tablespoon snipped chives**
- **1 tablespoon lemon juice**
- **¼ teaspoon salt**
- **Dash cayenne**

In saucepan add water to cover eggs. Bring to rapid boil over high heat. Reduce heat; cover and simmer for 15 to 20 minutes. Pour off hot water; fill saucepan with cold water and let stand 2 minutes. Drain and slightly cool eggs; remove shells. In saucepan place chicken livers with enough water to cover. Bring to boiling; reduce heat. Cover and simmer 10 minutes or till livers are tender. Drain livers; cool.

Halve eggs lengthwise; remove yolks. Arrange egg white halves on baking sheet lined with a towel. In blender container or food processor bowl place egg yolks, cooled chicken livers, mayonnaise or salad dressing, chives, lemon juice, salt, and cayenne. Process till smooth. Place egg yolk mixture in pastry bag. Pipe mixture into egg white halves (see photo). Cover and chill. Makes 16 appetizers.

Note: A blender or food processor is needed only for Liver-Stuffed Eggs. For the following variations, stir yolk mixture in a mixing bowl.

Anchovy-Stuffed Eggs

Prepare Liver-Stuffed Eggs as directed *except* add 1 tablespoon *anchovy paste* and ¼ teaspoon *worcestershire sauce* to the egg yolk mixture. Increase the mayonnaise or salad dressing to ¼ *cup* and omit chicken livers and salt. Fill egg white halves as above. If desired, garnish each with a rolled anchovy fillet.

Creamy Stuffed Eggs

Prepare Liver-Stuffed Eggs as directed *except* add 3 tablespoons *dairy sour cream* to the egg yolk mixture and omit the chicken livers. Fill egg white halves as above.

Stuffed Eggs Almondine

Prepare Liver-Stuffed Eggs as directed *except* increase the mayonnaise or salad dressing to ⅓ *cup* in the egg yolk mixture and omit the chicken livers. Fill egg white halves as directed. Garnish each stuffed egg with chopped *almonds*.

Caviar-Stuffed Eggs

Prepare Liver-Stuffed Eggs as directed *except* add 1 teaspoon *vinegar*, 1 teaspoon *prepared mustard*, and dash *pepper* to the egg yolk mixture. Increase mayonnaise or salad dressing to ⅓ *cup* and reduce salt to ⅛ *teaspoon*. Omit chicken livers, chives, lemon juice, and cayenne. Fill egg white halves as directed. Combine 2 tablespoons *capers*, drained, and 2 tablespoons *caviar* to garnish.

Arrange the egg white halves on a baking sheet lined with a towel. This prevents the eggs from sliding while being filled with the egg yolk mixture. Use a fancy tip on the pastry bag to make a decorative filling. Or, spoon yolk mixture into each egg white half.

French Omelet

Pictured on pages 42 and 43—

Tarragon-Asparagus Filling, Saucy Shrimp Filling, *or* **Fruit and Cheese Filling**

- 4 **eggs**
- 2 **tablespoons water**
- ¼ **teaspoon salt**
- ⅛ **teaspoon pepper**
- 2 **tablespoons butter** *or* **margarine**

Prepare desired filling and keep warm. Beat together eggs, water, salt, and pepper. In a 6- or 8-inch skillet with flared sides, heat *1 tablespoon* butter over medium heat till butter sizzles and browns slightly. Tilt the pan to coat the sides. Pour in *half* the egg mixture (about ½ cup) (step 1); cook over medium heat. As eggs set, run a spatula around edge of skillet, lifting eggs to allow uncooked portion to flow underneath (step 2). When eggs are set but still shiny, remove from heat. Spread *half* of the desired filling across the center (step 3). Using a spatula, carefully lift one-third of the cooked omelet over filling. Repeat with remaining one-third to overlap (step 4). Gently slide omelet to edge of skillet (step 5). Tilt skillet, then invert to roll omelet out onto warm serving plate (step 6). Repeat to make second omelet. Serves 2.

Tarragon-Asparagus Filling: In saucepan melt 2 tablespoons *butter or margarine*. Stir over very low heat till butter becomes dark brown but not burned. Stir in 1 teaspoon *lemon juice;* ⅛ teaspoon dried *tarragon,* crushed; dash *salt;* and dash *pepper.* Add 1 cup cooked sliced *asparagus;* heat through and keep warm.

Saucy Shrimp Filling: Melt 2 tablespoons *butter or margarine.* Cook 2 tablespoons thinly sliced *green onion* in butter till tender. Blend in 4 teaspoons *all-purpose flour,* ⅛ teaspoon dried *dillweed,* ⅛ teaspoon *salt,* and dash *pepper.* Add ½ cup *milk* all at once. Cook and stir till bubbly. Add ½ cup cooked and shelled *shrimp,* halved lengthwise. Heat through; remove from heat. Gradually stir mixture into 2 tablespoons *dairy sour cream.* Keep warm. Use some mixture to fill omelets; top omelets with remainder.

Fruit and Cheese Filling: In saucepan blend ½ cup *orange juice* and 2 teaspoons *lemon juice* into 2 teaspoons *cornstarch* and ⅛ teaspoon ground *nutmeg.* Cook and stir till bubbly. Keep warm. Combine ½ cup sliced fresh *strawberries* and 1 medium *orange,* peeled, sectioned, and halved. Fill omelets with fruit mixture. Spoon some sauce over fruit. Fold omelets. Spoon remaining sauce atop omelets; top with ½ cup shredded *gouda cheese.*

1 Cook half of the egg mixture over medium heat. Do not let skillet become too hot or the eggs will be overcooked and tough.

2 As eggs set, run a spatula around the edge of the skillet, lifting the eggs to allow the uncooked portion to flow underneath.

3 When eggs are set but top surface is still slightly shiny, remove the skillet from heat. Spread half of the desired filling across center of omelet.

4 *Using a metal spatula, carefully lift one-third of the cooked omelet and fold over filling in center. Repeat with remaining one-third to overlap.*

Puffy Omelet

The filling variations also can be used to fill a Puffy Omelet. Beaten egg whites give it a light, airy texture.

Puffy Omelet: Beat 4 *egg whites* till frothy. Add 2 tablespoons *water* and ¼ teaspoon *salt;* continue beating about 1½ minutes or till stiff peaks form. Beat 4 *egg yolks* at high speed of electric mixer about 5 minutes or till thick and lemon-colored. Fold egg yolks into egg whites. In a 10-inch skillet with an oven-proof handle, heat 1 tablespoon *butter or margarine* till a drop of water sizzles. Pour in egg mixture, mounding it slightly higher at the sides. Cook over low heat, uncovered, for 8 to 10 minutes or till eggs are puffed and set and bottom is golden brown. Place skillet in a 325° oven; bake for 10 minutes or till knife inserted near center comes out clean. Loosen sides of omelet with a metal spatula. Make a shallow cut across the omelet, cutting slightly off-center. Spread desired filling on larger half. Tilt pan. Fold smaller half over larger half. Using spatula, slip omelet onto hot platter. Makes 2 servings.

5 *Gently slide filled omelet to the edge of skillet opposite handle. Hold skillet at an angle to a warmed serving plate.*

6 *To remove omelet, tilt pan, then invert so that omelet rolls out onto plate. (Or, slide the omelet out of pan so that overlapped edges remain on top.)*

Shrimp-Almond Quiche

Quiche is an open-faced tart filled with an un-sweetened custard that is flavored with cheese, seafood, or meat. This one is pictured on pages 42 and 43—

Pastry for Single-Crust Pie (see recipe, page 88)
½ **cup chopped fresh mushrooms**
¼ **cup sliced green onion**
1 **tablespoon butter** *or* **margarine**
3 **beaten eggs**
1½ **cups light cream**
2 **tablespoons snipped parsley**
1 **tablespoon all-purpose flour**
1 **teaspoon salt**
1 **teaspoon lemon juice**
¼ **teaspoon dijon-style mustard**
Dash pepper
½ **cup shredded gruyère** *or* **Swiss cheese**
2 **tablespoons dry white wine**
1 **cup fresh** *or* **frozen shelled shrimp, cooked and halved lengthwise**
¼ **cup toasted, slivered almonds**

Prepare pastry. On floured surface, roll out pastry till dough is about ⅛ inch thick. Line a 9-inch quiche dish or pie plate. Trim pastry ½ to 1 inch beyond edge of dish; fold excess under (step 1). Flute edge of pastry high (step 2). Line pastry with a double thickness of heavy-duty foil; fill with dry beans (step 3). Bake in 450° oven for 5 minutes. Carefully remove the beans and foil. Bake 5 to 7 minutes more or till pastry is golden. Remove from oven; reduce oven temperature to 325°. (Pastry shell should be hot when filled; do not partially bake it ahead of time.)

Cook mushrooms and green onion in butter till onion is tender but not brown. In bowl combine eggs, cream, parsley, flour, salt, lemon juice, mustard, and pepper using a wire whisk. Stir in mushroom-onion mixture, cheese, and wine. Place hot pastry shell on oven rack. Arrange halved shrimp in bottom of pastry shell. Pour egg mixture into shell; sprinkle almonds atop. If necessary, cover edge of crust with foil to prevent overbrowning. Bake in 325° oven for 30 to 35 minutes or till knife inserted near center comes out clean. Let stand 10 minutes before serving; cut into wedges. Serves 6.

1 Use kitchen shears or a sharp knife to trim the edge of the pastry ½ to 1 inch beyond the edge of the dish. Fold under the extra pastry to build up the edge, as shown.

2 Flute entire edge of pastry. Press dough with the forefinger of one hand (from outside of dish) against the thumb and forefinger of the other hand (placed inside the dish), following the design of the quiche dish.

3 Line the pastry with a double thickness of heavy-duty foil; fill with dry beans. This prevents the pastry from puffing up or shrinking while baking.

Hollandaise Sauce

Egg yolk-thickened sauces require full attention, since they curdle easily if heated too quickly or cooked too long. Béarnaise Sauce is similar to Hollandaise but has added herbs—

4 egg yolks
½ cup butter, softened
2 to 3 tablespoons lemon juice
Dash salt
Dash white pepper

Place egg yolks and *one-third* of the butter in top of double boiler. Cook over boiling water till butter melts, stirring rapidly. (Water in bottom of double boiler should not touch top pan.) Add a *second third* of the butter and continue stirring. As butter melts and mixture thickens, add remaining butter, stirring constantly. When butter is melted, remove top pan from water; using a wooden spoon, stir rapidly for 2 minutes. Stir in the lemon juice, 1 teaspoon at a time. Season with salt and white pepper. Heat and stir again over boiling water 2 to 3 minutes or till thickened. Remove from heat at once. The sauce should be thick but pourable (step 1). (If sauce curdles, immediately beat in 1 or 2 tablespoons boiling water.) Serve hot over vegetables, poultry, fish, or eggs. Makes 1 cup.

Food processor directions: Place steel blade in work bowl; add the egg yolks, lemon juice, and pepper. Omit salt. Process with on/off turns just till blended. Heat butter almost to boiling. With machine running, gradually pour hot butter through feed tube in a steady stream (step 2). Process about 3 minutes or till thick and fluffy. Scrape down sides of bowl as needed. Serve immediately or keep warm in a double boiler set over hot (not boiling) water.

Sauce Mousseline

Prepare Hollandaise Sauce as above; cool. Beat ½ cup *whipping cream* till soft peaks form; fold into cooled Hollandaise Sauce. To serve, spoon sauce over hot cooked vegetables. Broil 2 to 3 inches from heat for a few seconds or till lightly browned and bubbly. Serve immediately.

1 *Heat, stirring constantly, for 2 to 3 minutes or till thickened. Remove from heat at once. The finished sauce should be thick but pourable, as shown.*

2 *When making Hollandaise Sauce in the food processor, change the order of assembling ingredients. Process eggs and lemon juice till smooth, then add melted butter.*

Béarnaise Sauce

Mix 3 tablespoons *white wine vinegar*; 1 teaspoon finely chopped *shallot or onion*; 4 whole *black peppercorns*, crushed; dash dried *tarragon*, crushed; and dash dried *chervil*, crushed. Simmer about 30 seconds. Strain; discard solids. Add 1 tablespoon cold *water* to the herb liquid. Prepare Hollandaise Sauce as above *except* combine the egg yolks and only *2 tablespoons* of the butter in top of double boiler. Slowly add herb liquid. Place over gently boiling water. Cook and stir till butter melts and sauce begins to thicken. Add remaining butter, 2 tablespoons at a time, while stirring constantly. Cook and stir till sauce is the consistency of thick cream. Remove from heat. Stir in ¼ teaspoon dried *tarragon*, crushed, and the dash salt. Omit lemon juice and pepper. Serve over cooked meat, poultry, or fish. Makes ¾ cup.

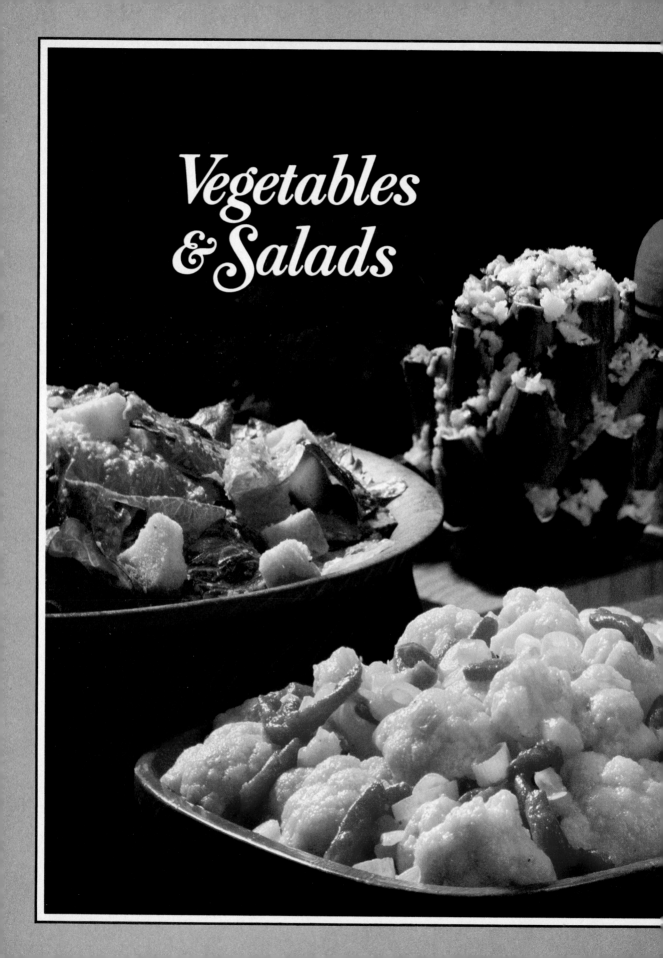

Vegetables & Salads

These vegetable and salad accompaniments make a gourmet meal in themselves. Piquant *Curried Cauliflower* (see recipe, page 60) is shown alongside *Vegetable Vinaigrette* (see recipe, page 58). Tangy *Baked Potato Puffs* (see recipe, page 59) are prepared in individual casseroles. Finally, steamed *Stuffed Artichokes* (see recipe, page 54) and classic *Caesar Salad* (see recipe, page 55) are two gourmet traditions.

Stuffed Artichokes

Stuffed whole artichokes create a stylish vegetable accompaniment. Pictured on pages 52 and 53 —

 4 **medium artichokes**
    Lemon juice
 2 **cups chopped fresh mushrooms** *or* **two 4-ounce cans mushroom stems and pieces, drained and chopped**
 ½ **cup sliced green onion**
 ½ **cup butter** *or* **margarine**
 3 **cups soft bread crumbs (4 slices)**
 ½ **cup grated parmesan** *or* **romano cheese**
 ¼ **cup snipped parsley**
 1 **teaspoon dried thyme, crushed**
    Green onion fans (optional)
    Lemon twists (optional)

Remove stems and loose outer leaves from artichokes. Cut off 1 inch from tops; snip off sharp leaf tips (step 1). Brush cut edges with lemon juice. Place artichokes in steamer basket. Place over boiling water. Cover and steam for 30 to 40 minutes or till a leaf pulls out easily. (Add additional boiling water, if necessary.) Remove artichokes; set aside till cool enough to handle. Remove center leaves and choke (step 2).

For stuffing, in skillet cook fresh mushrooms and green onion in butter or margarine till tender (reserve canned mushrooms). Continue cooking vegetable mixture, uncovered, till excess liquid evaporates. Remove from heat. Stir in the canned mushrooms (if using canned), bread crumbs, parmesan or romano cheese, snipped parsley, and thyme.

Spread artichoke leaves slightly. Spoon stuffing into center of each artichoke and behind each large leaf (step 3). Return artichokes to steamer basket. Place over boiling water. Cover and steam for 10 to 15 minutes or till stuffing is heated through. Garnish serving platter with green onion fans and lemon twists, if desired. Makes 4 servings.

1 With a sharp knife, remove bottom stems so artichokes sit flat. Remove loose outer leaves. Cut off 1 inch from the tops of the artichokes. Snip off the sharp leaf tips with kitchen scissors, as shown. Brush lemon juice on the cut edges to prevent the surfaces from browning.

2 When cooked artichokes are cool enough to handle, pull out the center leaves. Scoop out the fuzzy choke with a spoon. Discard the choke.

3 To stuff artichokes, spread leaves apart slightly. Fill center of each artichoke with stuffing. Spoon additional stuffing behind each large leaf.

Caesar Salad

Serve Caesar Salad immediately after the ingredients are combined. You can serve it already assembled, or toss it together right at the table. Pictured on pages 52 and 53—

- **1 medium head romaine**
- **1 egg**
- **1 clove garlic, halved**
- **3 anchovy fillets**
- **3 tablespoons olive oil**
- **½ lemon**
- **Few dashes worcestershire sauce**
- **½ cup Garlic Croutons**
- **¼ cup grated parmesan cheese**
- **Whole black pepper**

Cut the bottom core from romaine and discard. Wash romaine leaves under cold running water. Discard any discolored or wilted leaves. Gently pat dry with paper toweling or clean kitchen towel. Place loosely in plastic bag; chill to crisp.

Cut lengthwise along both sides of the midrib of romaine leaves (step 1); remove and discard midribs. Tear romaine leaves into bite-size pieces (should have about 6 cups). Meanwhile, allow egg to come to room temperature. To coddle egg, place whole egg in saucepan of boiling water; remove from heat. Let stand 1 minute. Remove egg from water; cool slightly.

Rub large wooden salad bowl with cut garlic clove; discard garlic. In bottom of bowl combine anchovy fillets and olive oil. Using a fork or the back of a spoon, mash till smooth. Squeeze lemon over the mixture; blend in worcestershire sauce. Break coddled egg into bowl; mix till dressing becomes creamy (step 2). Add torn romaine; toss to coat. Sprinkle with Garlic Croutons and parmesan cheese. Grind pepper over salad; toss gently to mix. Serves 6.

Garlic Croutons: Gradually blend ¼ cup *cooking oil* into ¼ cup softened *butter or margarine*. Stir in 2 cloves *garlic*, finely minced. Using 8 to 10 slices *French bread*, cut ½ inch thick, *or* 8 slices firm-textured *white bread*, brush butter mixture on both sides of bread. Cut bread into ½-inch cubes. Spread cubes in a large shallow baking pan. Heat in 300° oven for 20 to 25 minutes or till bread is dry and crisp, stirring at least once. Cool. Store in covered container in refrigerator. Makes 3 to 4 cups.

1 With sharp knife or kitchen scissors, cut lengthwise along both sides of the heavy midrib of each romaine leaf. Remove and discard the midribs. Tear the romaine leaves into bite-size pieces. Tearing exposes the juicy inner surfaces and allows the greens to better absorb the dressing.

2 Break the coddled egg into the salad bowl. Using a fork or the back of a spoon, mix the egg into the anchovy mixture until the dressing becomes creamy.

Crab-Avocado Salads

Avocados range in color from green to almost black, but the ripeness test is the same for all varieties. The fruit should yield to gentle pressure when ready to eat. Store firm avocados at room temperature to ripen quickly; refrigerate to ripen slowly—

- **5 medium avocados**
- **2 teaspoons lemon juice**
- **¼ cup dairy sour cream**
- **2 tablespoons mayonnaise *or* salad dressing**
- **¼ teaspoon salt**
- **¼ teaspoon dry mustard**
- **1 6-ounce can crab meat, chilled, drained, flaked, and cartilage removed**
- **½ cup thinly sliced celery**
- **Toasted, slivered almonds**
- **Lettuce**

Peel and dice one of the avocados; sprinkle with *1 teaspoon* of the lemon juice. Set aside. Cut the remaining avocados in half lengthwise; twist gently and separate. Tap seed with sharp edge of knife; twist and lift, or gently pry out seed.

Scoop out avocado pulp, leaving a ¼-inch shell (step 1). Sprinkle avocado pulp with the remaining 1 teaspoon lemon juice. Brush cut surface of avocado shells with additional lemon juice. Trim a thin slice from the bottom of each shell (step 2). Set avocado shells aside.

Mash the avocado pulp. Add sour cream, mayonnaise or salad dressing, salt, and dry mustard; beat till smooth. Combine crab meat and celery; toss with sour cream mixture. Gently fold in the reserved diced avocado. Fill the avocado shells with crab mixture. Sprinkle with toasted slivered almonds. Serve immediately on individual lettuce-lined salad plates. Makes 4 servings.

1 Hold avocado half firmly in the palm of your hand. With a serving spoon, scoop out the pulp, leaving a ¼-inch shell. Sprinkle the avocado pulp with 1 teaspoon lemon juice to prevent darkening.

2 Trim a thin slice from the bottom of each avocado half with a sharp knife so shells will sit flat. Fill avocado halves with crab salad mixture.

Vichyssoise
(Vee-she-SWAHZ)

Prepare this elegant first-course soup ahead of time to chill thoroughly—

- **2 leeks**
- **1 small onion, sliced**
- **2 tablespoons butter *or* margarine**
- **3 small potatoes, peeled and sliced (2½ cups)**
- **2 cups Chicken Stock (see recipe, page 29)**
- **1½ cups milk**
- **White pepper**
- **1 cup whipping cream**
- **Snipped chives**

Wash leeks to remove sand. Trim roots and tops; discard. Slice the white portion of leeks (step 1). In a 2-quart saucepan cook leeks and onion in butter or margarine till vegetables are tender but not brown. Stir in sliced potatoes, Chicken Stock, and 1 teaspoon *salt*. Bring to boiling. Reduce heat; cover and simmer for 35 to 40 minutes or till potatoes are very tender.

Place *half* of the mixture in blender container or food processor bowl; cover and blend till mixture is smooth. Pour into a bowl. Repeat with remaining mixture. Return all of the mixture to saucepan; stir in milk. Season to taste with white pepper and salt. Bring to boiling, stirring frequently. Cool. Stir in whipping cream. Cover and chill thoroughly before serving. If desired, serve in individual bowls set in larger bowls filled with crushed ice. Garnish with snipped chives (step 2). Makes 4 to 6 servings.

Cold Soups

Vichyssoise and other cold soups are often served as appetizers; offer ½- to ¾-cup servings. Be sure to serve cold soups very cold in chilled cups, sherbet dishes, or bowls. Or, surround serving bowls with crushed ice in glass icers.

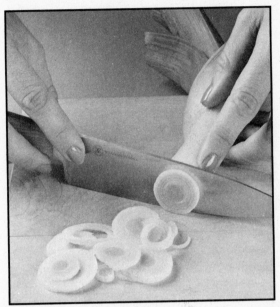

1 Thinly slice the white portion of both leeks. Only this white portion is used in the soup. After slicing both leeks, you should have about ⅔ cup.

2 Set individual servings of soup in larger bowls filled with crushed ice to keep the soup very cold. Garnish with snipped chives to add color and contribute to the overall flavor of the soup.

Vegetable Vinaigrette

Asparagus, tomatoes, mushrooms, and onion marinate in a vinaigrette dressing in this dish pictured on pages 52 and 53—

¾ pound **fresh asparagus** *or* one 8-ounce package **frozen asparagus spears**
½ cup **salad oil**
2 tablespoons **white wine vinegar**
2 tablespoons **lemon juice**
2 teaspoons **snipped fresh dill** *or* ½ teaspoon **dried dillweed**
1½ teaspoons **sugar**
1 teaspoon **paprika**
½ teaspoon **salt**
½ teaspoon **dry mustard**
3 medium **tomatoes, peeled and thinly sliced**
1 cup **sliced fresh mushrooms**
1 small **onion, thinly sliced and separated into rings**
Lettuce

Wash fresh asparagus and scrape off scales with a knife. Break off woody bases at point where spears snap easily (step 1). With string, fasten whole spears in a bundle (step 2). Stand asparagus upright in a deep kettle, letting tips extend 2 to 3 inches above boiling salted water (step 3). Cook, covered, for 8 to 12 minutes or till spears are crisp-tender. (Or, cook frozen asparagus according to package directions.) Drain asparagus.

For dressing, in screw-top jar combine salad oil, vinegar, lemon juice, dill, sugar, paprika, salt, and dry mustard. Cover and shake well.

Place asparagus, tomatoes, mushrooms, and onion in shallow dish. Pour dressing over all. Cover; refrigerate several hours or overnight, spooning dressing over vegetables occasionally.

To serve, lift vegetables from dressing with slotted spoon. Arrange vegetables on lettuce-lined platter or transfer to serving bowl; spoon some of the dressing over vegetables. Pass remaining dressing. Makes 6 servings.

1 Wash asparagus spears and scrape off scales with a knife. Remove woody bases by breaking stalks. Stalks will snap easily where tender parts begin.

2 For easier handling, fasten fresh asparagus spears in a bundle. Secure with string just below the tips and again near the bases.

3 Place asparagus, tips up, in a deep narrow kettle filled with boiling salted water. If desired, place the spears on a rack, as shown. Asparagus tips should extend 2 to 3 inches above the water. If the tips are immersed in the water, they will overcook.

Baked Potato Puffs

Crème Fraîche is a tangy mixture of whipping cream and cultured buttermilk that is often used in French cooking. Make it a day ahead of time or use sour cream instead. This vegetable recipe is pictured on pages 52 and 53—

3 medium potatoes, peeled and cubed (1 pound)
⅓ cup light cream
3 tablespoons Crème Fraîche *or* dairy sour cream
2 tablespoons grated parmesan cheese
2 tablespoons snipped chives
2 teaspoons snipped fresh basil *or* ½ teaspoon dried basil, crushed
¼ teaspoon salt
⅛ teaspoon pepper
3 egg yolks
3 egg whites
2 tablespoons butter *or* margarine, melted
Grated parmesan cheese

Cook potatoes in boiling water about 10 minutes or till tender; drain and mash (should have 2 cups mashed potatoes). In saucepan combine mashed potatoes, light cream, and Crème Fraîche or sour cream. Stir over low heat till very hot. Remove from heat. Add 2 tablespoons parmesan cheese, chives, basil, salt, and pepper; mix well. Add egg yolks, one at a time, beating well after each addition (step 1). Beat egg whites to stiff peaks. Fold a little of the beaten egg whites into the potato mixture; fold the lightened potato mixture back into the remaining egg whites (step 2). Turn mixture into 6 individual 1-cup baking dishes. Brush a little melted butter atop each. Sprinkle with additional parmesan cheese. Bake in 350° oven about 25 minutes or till lightly browned. Serve immediately. Makes 6 servings.

Crème Fraîche: In small saucepan heat 2 cups *whipping cream* to between 90° and 100°. Pour into small bowl. Stir in ¼ cup *cultured buttermilk*. Cover and let stand at room temperature for 18 to 24 hours or till mixture is thickened. Do not stir. Store in covered container in refrigerator up to one week. Makes 2 cups.

1 Add egg yolks, one at a time, beating well after each addition. After the last egg yolk is beaten in, the mixture should be smooth and free of lumps.

2 Use a wooden spoon to fold a small amount of stiff-beaten egg whites into the potato mixture. Gently fold the lightened potato mixture back into the remaining egg whites. To fold, use a circular down-up-and-over motion, while turning the bowl.

Curried Cauliflower

Use the smaller amount of curry for a milder-seasoned food. Pictured on pages 52 and 53—

  1 large head cauliflower
  ¼ cup sliced green onion
  ¼ to ½ teaspoon curry powder
  ¼ cup butter *or* margarine
  2 teaspoons lemon juice
  ½ teaspoon salt
  ⅛ teaspoon pepper
  1 2-ounce jar sliced pimiento, drained

Rinse cauliflower under cold water and remove the outer green leaves. Using a sharp knife, cut out the woody stem. Break cauliflower into flowerets (step 1). Place flowerets in steamer basket. Place basket over boiling water (step 2). Cover and steam for 22 minutes or just till tender. (Add more boiling water, if necessary.)

Meanwhile, in skillet cook green onion with curry powder in butter or margarine till onion is tender. Add lemon juice, salt, and pepper. Stir in sliced pimiento. Add steamed cauliflower and stir gently to mix. Turn into serving bowl; spoon juices from skillet over vegetable mixture. Makes 4 to 6 servings.

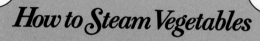

How to Steam Vegetables

Ever try steam cooking? It's a method of cooking that preserves the natural flavor and nutrients of fresh vegetables.

If you have a self-adjusting stainless steel basket, you can turn almost any saucepan into a vegetable steamer. To steam vegetables, place uniform-size pieces in the steamer basket. The basket prevents the vegetables from coming in contact with the liquid. In a saucepan bring water to boiling. Place the basket of vegetables over the boiling water, making sure the water doesn't touch the basket. Cover saucepan and steam vegetables till crisp-tender. Reduce heat after the steaming process starts. During cooking, test vegetables as little as possible so steam won't escape. Check the water level, refilling with boiling water if necessary.

1 Break cauliflower into small pieces called flowerets. If necessary, use a sharp knife to help loosen the flowerets. A large head of cauliflower will yield about 4 cups of flowerets.

2 Place the basket of flowerets over (but not touching) boiling water in a saucepan. Cover the saucepan and steam for 22 minutes. To test for doneness, insert a fork in the stalk portion of several flowerets. The cauliflower should still be slightly crisp, yet tender.

Mayonnaise

Having homemade Mayonnaise on hand for your favorite recipes is a real luxury. Be sure to add the oil very gradually—

- 1 teaspoon salt
- ½ teaspoon dry mustard
- ¼ teaspoon paprika
  Dash cayenne
- 2 egg yolks
- 2 tablespoons vinegar
- 2 cups salad oil
- 2 tablespoons lemon juice

In small mixer bowl combine salt, dry mustard, paprika, and cayenne. Add egg yolks and vinegar; beat mixture at medium speed of electric mixer till blended. Add the salad oil, 1 teaspoon at a time, beating constantly. Continue adding oil 1 teaspoon at a time and beating mixture till only ¼ cup oil has been added (step 1). While continuing to beat, add more salad oil in a thin, steady stream till all but ½ cup has been added (step 2). Alternate adding the remaining ½ cup salad oil with the lemon juice (step 3). Store in a tightly covered jar in the refrigerator. Label and date the jar before storing. Since homemade Mayonnaise doesn't contain preservatives, you should use it within 4 weeks. Makes 2 cups.

Food processor directions: Place steel blade in work bowl; add egg yolks, vinegar, lemon juice, salt, dry mustard, paprika, and cayenne. Process just till all ingredients are well blended. With machine running, add oil quickly through feed tube, pouring in a steady stream. Process to desired thickness. Makes 2 cups.

Herb Mayonnaise

Mix 1 cup *mayonnaise*; 2 tablespoons finely chopped *onion*; 1 tablespoon *lemon juice*; 1 tablespoon *dry sherry*; 1 clove *garlic*, minced; 1 teaspoon *worcestershire sauce*; and ½ teaspoon dried *mixed salad herbs*, crushed. Makes 1¼ cups.

Chive Mayonnaise

Mix 1 cup *mayonnaise*, ¼ cup snipped *chives*, 1 tablespoon *lemon juice*, 2 teaspoons *tarragon vinegar*, and dash *salt*. Makes 1¼ cups.

1 Add salad oil to the egg mixture, 1 teaspoon at a time, beating constantly. Continue beating mixture till ¼ cup oil has been added. If oil is added to the yolk mixture too rapidly, an emulsion will not form. Instead, the oil will separate out.

2 While continuing to beat, add more of the salad oil by pouring in a thin, steady stream, till all but ½ cup has been added.

3 Alternate adding the last ½ cup oil with the lemon juice, beating at medium speed till thoroughly blended.

Breads, Rice, & Pasta

Tender, warm-from-the-oven breads are always tempting. And rice and pasta become special side dishes when you add vegetables and seasonings. Linguine in a rich sauce with broccoli makes *Pasta Verde* (see recipe, page 69). Creamy *Saffron Risotto* (see recipe, page 70) abounds with delicate flavors. And on the bread server are flaky *Croissants* (see recipe, pages 66 and 67), *Brioche*, a rich French yeast roll (see recipe, page 64), and satisfying *Pecan Popovers* (see recipe, page 65).

Brioche

(Bree-OSH)

These rich French yeast rolls shaped with a topknot are pictured on pages 62 and 63—

- **1 package active dry yeast**
- **¼ cup warm water (110° to 115°)**
- **½ cup butter *or* margarine**
- **⅓ cup sugar**
- **½ teaspoon salt**
- **4 cups all-purpose flour**
- **½ cup milk**
- **4 eggs**
- **1 tablespoon water**

Soften yeast in ¼ cup warm water. Cream butter or margarine, sugar, and salt. Add *1 cup* of the flour and the milk to creamed mixture. Separate *one* of the eggs; set egg white aside. Combine yolk and the remaining 3 eggs; add to creamed mixture. Add softened yeast; beat well. Stir in the remaining flour till dough is smooth. Turn into greased bowl. Cover; let rise in warm place till double (about 2 hours). Refrigerate dough overnight.

Stir dough down; turn out onto lightly floured surface. Divide into quarters; set one aside. Divide each remaining quarter into 6 pieces, making a total of 18. Form each piece into a ball (step 1). Place each in a greased individual brioche pan.* Divide reserved dough into 18 pieces; shape into balls. Make an indentation in each large ball (step 2). Press a small ball into each indentation. Combine reserved egg white and 1 tablespoon water; brush over rolls. Cover; let rise till nearly double (40 to 45 minutes). Bake in 375° oven about 15 minutes, brushing again after 7 minutes. Makes 18.

*If desired, use muffin pans instead of individual brioche pans. Prepare dough and divide into quarters as above; set one aside. Divide each remaining quarter into 8 pieces, making a total of 24. Form into balls; place in 24 greased muffin cups. Divide reserved dough into 24 pieces; shape into balls. Press each into indentation in large ball. Brush with egg white mixture. Let rise; bake as directed. Makes 24.

1 With floured hands, shape each piece of dough into a ball. Pull the edges under to make a smooth top, as shown. Place each ball, smooth side up, in a greased brioche pan or muffin cup.

2 With floured finger, make an indentation in the center of each large ball. Gently press a small ball into the indentation in each large ball. Combine egg white and water, brush over rolls.

Popovers

Puffy Pecan Popovers with a crusty outer shell and a tender lining are pictured on pages 62 and 63—

- 1½ **teaspoons shortening**
- 2 **beaten eggs**
- 1 **cup milk**
- 1 **tablespoon cooking oil**
- 1 **cup all-purpose flour**
- ½ **teaspoon salt**

Grease six 6-ounce custard cups with ¼ *teaspoon* of the shortening for *each* cup. Place custard cups on a 15x10x1-inch baking pan or baking sheet and place in oven; preheat oven to 450°. Meanwhile, in a 4-cup liquid measure or mixing bowl combine beaten eggs, milk, and cooking oil. Add flour and salt. Beat with electric mixer or rotary beater till mixture is smooth.

Remove pan from oven. Fill the hot custard cups *half* full (step 1). Return to oven. Bake in 450° oven for 20 minutes. Reduce oven temperature to 350° and bake 15 to 20 minutes more or till popovers are *very* firm. (If popovers brown too quickly, turn off oven and finish baking in the cooling oven till very firm.) A few minutes before removing from oven, prick each popover with a fork to let steam escape (step 2). Serve hot. Makes 6 popovers.

Note: If you like popovers dry and crisp, turn off the oven after popovers are completely baked. Leave them in oven 30 minutes more with door ajar.

Pecan Popovers

Prepare Popover batter as above *except* stir ¼ cup finely chopped *pecans* into the batter.

Whole Wheat Popovers

Prepare Popover batter as above *except* use only ⅔ cup all-purpose flour and add ⅓ cup *whole wheat flour*.

Cinnamon Popovers

Prepare Popover batter as above *except* add 1 teaspoon ground *cinnamon* to the egg mixture.

1 Carefully pour the batter from liquid measure or mixing bowl, filling each hot custard cup only half full. Return to 450° oven.

2 Bake popovers till **very** firm. A few minutes before removing from oven, prick each popover with a fork to allow steam to escape. This prevents popovers from becoming soggy.

Yorkshire Pudding

Prepare Yorkshire Pudding to accompany roast beef by following the mixing technique for making Popovers.

In a 15½x10½x2-inch roasting pan retain ¼ cup *roast beef pan drippings*. Combine 4 beaten *eggs* and 2 cups *milk*. Add 2 cups *all-purpose flour* and 1 teaspoon *salt*; beat till smooth. Pour into pan atop drippings. Bake in 400° oven about 40 minutes. Cut into squares; serve immediately.

Croissants

(Kwa-SAWNTS)

Sealing chilled butter between layers of dough contributes to the flaky texture of these French crescent-shaped rolls. Pictured on pages 62 and 63—

1½	cups butter *or* margarine
⅓	cup all-purpose flour
2	packages active dry yeast
½	cup warm water (110° to 115°)
¾	cup milk
¼	cup sugar
1	teaspoon salt
1	egg
3¾ to 4¼	cups all-purpose flour
1	egg yolk
1	tablespoon milk

Cream butter or margarine with ⅓ cup flour. Roll butter mixture into a 12x6-inch rectangle (step 1). Chill at least 1 hour.

Soften yeast in warm water. Heat ¾ cup milk, sugar, and salt till sugar dissolves. Cool to lukewarm; turn into large mixing bowl. Add softened yeast and 1 egg; beat well.

Stir in *2 cups* of the flour; beat well. Stir in as much of the remaining flour as you can mix in with a spoon. Turn dough out onto lightly floured surface. Knead in enough of the remaining flour to make a moderately soft dough that is smooth and elastic (3 to 5 minutes total). Cover and let rest 10 minutes.

Roll dough into a 14-inch square. Place *chilled* butter mixture on *half* of dough (step 2). Fold over other half of dough and seal edges (step 3). Roll into a 21x12-inch rectangle; chill. Fold into thirds; seal edges (step 4). Roll into a 21x12-inch rectangle (step 5). Fold and roll twice more. Chill after each rolling. Fold into thirds to 12x7 inches. Cover with clear plastic wrap and chill several hours or overnight.

Cut dough crosswise into fourths. Roll each fourth into a 12-inch circle. Cut each circle into 12 wedges. Roll up each wedge loosely, starting from wide end (step 6).

Place, point down, on *ungreased* baking sheets; curve ends. Cover; let rise till nearly double (30 to 45 minutes). Beat egg yolk with 1 tablespoon milk; brush over rolls. Bake in 375° oven for 12 to 15 minutes or till golden. Remove from baking sheets. Serve warm. Makes 48.

1 On baking sheet, roll out the butter-flour mixture between two sheets of waxed paper. Using a ruler as a guide, roll into a 12x6-inch rectangle. Chill well.

2 On lightly floured surface, roll out dough into a 14-inch square. If dough sticks to rolling pin, lightly rub rolling pin with flour. Place chilled butter mixture on half of the dough, as shown.

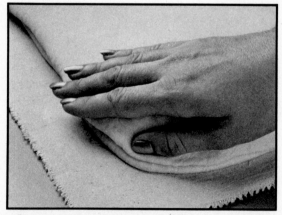

3 Carefully lift the other half of dough and lay over butter mixture to cover. With hand, seal all three edges of dough. Sealing butter between layers of dough makes rolls flaky.

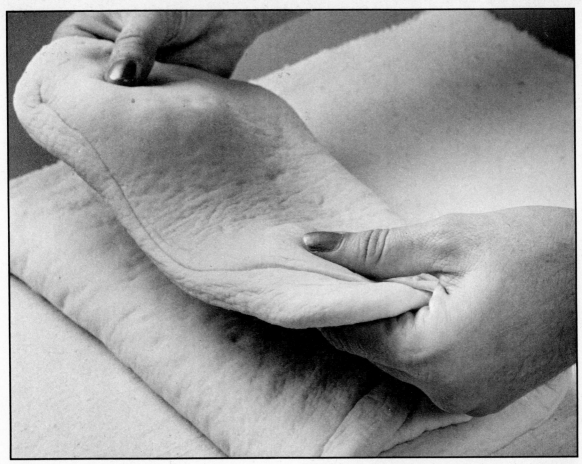

4 *Roll out dough into a 21x12-inch rectangle. Chill well. Gently lift the dough, without stretching, and fold into thirds. Stretch dough gently to even the layers. Seal edges.*

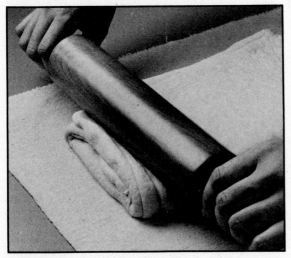

5 *On the lightly floured surface, roll out the three-layer piece of dough into a 21x12-inch rectangle. Repeat folding and rolling the dough two more times. Chill dough after each rolling to solidify butter.*

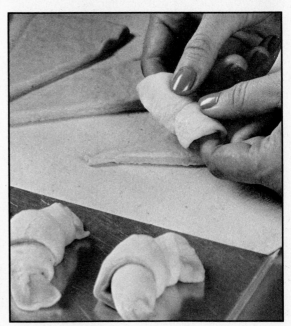

6 *Roll each fourth of dough into a 12-inch circle. Cut each into 12 wedges. Begin at wide end of wedge and roll loosely toward point. Place, point down, on ungreased baking sheet. Curve slightly.*

Wild Rice and Broccoli Pilaf

1 cup wild rice
2 cups Chicken Stock (see recipe, page 29)
¼ cup dry sherry
¾ cup sliced fresh mushrooms
¾ cup sliced celery
2 tablespoons sliced green onion
2 tablespoons butter *or* margarine
2 tablespoons chopped pimiento
½ teaspoon salt
¼ teaspoon dried thyme, crushed
Dash pepper
½ pound fresh broccoli *or* one 10-ounce package frozen cut broccoli
Lemon wedges (optional)

Run cold water over rice in a strainer for 1 to 2 minutes, lifting rice with fingers to rinse well (step 1). In saucepan combine rice, Chicken Stock, and sherry. Bring to boiling; reduce heat. Cover and simmer for 40 minutes. Do not drain.

Meanwhile, cook mushrooms, celery, and green onion in butter or margarine about 5 minutes or till celery is crisp-tender. Remove from heat. Add pimiento, salt, thyme, and pepper; toss to mix. Stir vegetable mixture into rice and turn into a 1½-quart casserole. Cover and bake in 325° oven for 25 minutes, stirring once.

Meanwhile, cut fresh broccoli stalks lengthwise into uniform spears, following the branching lines. Cut off buds and set aside. Cut the remaining part of spears into 1-inch pieces. In covered saucepan cook broccoli pieces in boiling salted water for 10 to 12 minutes or just till tender, adding reserved broccoli buds the last 5 minutes. (Or, cook frozen broccoli according to package directions.) Drain. Stir cooked broccoli into rice mixture (step 2). Continue baking, covered, for 10 to 15 minutes more or till rice is tender. Garnish with lemon wedges, if desired. Makes 6 servings.

1 To rinse wild rice, place rice in a fine-mesh strainer. Run cold water over rice for 1 to 2 minutes. Lift the rice with your fingers while rinsing it to help remove any particles.

2 Cook fresh or frozen broccoli just till tender; drain. Carefully stir broccoli into the partially cooked rice mixture. Adding the broccoli during the last several minutes of baking prevents it from overcooking.

Pasta Verde

(PAS-ta VARE-day)

Try your hand at tossing this rich vegetable-pasta dish, pictured on pages 62 and 63—

 4 **eggs**
 ¼ **cup whipping cream**
 3 **tablespoons butter** *or* **margarine**
 1½ **cups sliced fresh mushrooms**
 ½ **cup finely chopped onion**
 3 **tablespoons butter** *or* **margarine**
 1 **10-ounce package frozen chopped broccoli** *or* **spinach, cooked and well drained**
 12 **ounces hot cooked linguine, fettucini,** *or* **other pasta**
 1 **cup grated parmesan cheese**
 Dash pepper

Let eggs, whipping cream, and 3 tablespoons butter or margarine stand at room temperature for 2 to 3 hours. In skillet cook mushrooms and onion in the remaining 3 tablespoons butter or margarine till onion is tender. Stir in cooked broccoli or spinach; heat through. Beat together eggs and whipping cream just till blended.

Toss pasta with the softened butter or margarine. Pour egg mixture over and toss till pasta is well coated (step 1). Add broccoli or spinach mixture, parmesan cheese, and pepper; toss to mix (step 2). Serve immediately. Serves 8.

1 In small mixing bowl beat together eggs and whipping cream with a fork just till blended. Pour egg mixture over the buttered hot pasta. Toss quickly with two forks till pasta is well coated. The heat from the pasta cooks the eggs.

Cooking Pasta

To cook pasta, fill a large saucepan with 2 quarts *water* and 2 teaspoons *salt* for each 6 ounces *pasta*. Bring to a vigorous rolling boil. Add pasta a little at a time so water does not stop boiling. Reduce heat slightly; continue boiling, uncovered, till pasta is tender but still slightly firm, a stage Italians call *al dente* (to the tooth). Stir occasionally to prevent pasta from sticking together.

When pasta is done, drain in a colander. *Do not rinse.* Transfer pasta to a warm serving dish. Serve immediately.

2 Add warm broccoli or spinach mixture, parmesan cheese, and pepper to the coated pasta. Toss quickly with two forks till ingredients are well distributed.

Saffron Risotto
(SAFF-run Ruh-SOT-o)

In certain northern areas of Italy, rice is as important a staple as pasta. There are many ways to prepare rice, but risotto, which is rice cooked in a seasoned broth until the mixture is creamy, is the most common and popular. This delicate side dish is pictured on pages 62 and 63—

¼ **cup thinly sliced leek *or* chopped onion**
¼ **cup chopped sweet red pepper**
2 **tablespoons butter *or* margarine**
3 **cups Chicken Stock (see recipe, page 29)**
1 **cup short, medium, *or* long grain rice**
½ **cup finely chopped carrot**
1 **teaspoon salt**
⅛ **teaspoon thread saffron, crushed**
  Dash pepper
1 **medium tomato, peeled, seeded, and chopped**
2 **tablespoons snipped Italian parsley *or* parsley**
  Carrot spirals (optional)
  Italian parsley *or* parsley sprigs (optional)
  Grated parmesan *or* romano cheese (optional)

In a 3-quart saucepan cook sliced leek or chopped onion and red pepper in butter or margarine till leek is tender but not brown. Stir in Chicken Stock, *uncooked* rice, carrot, salt, saffron, and pepper. Bring mixture to a rolling boil; reduce heat to low. Cover and simmer for 15 minutes; remove from heat (step 1).

Stir in chopped tomato and 2 tablespoons snipped parsley. Cover and let stand for 5 to 8 minutes or just till rice is tender (step 2). Garnish with carrot spirals and parsley sprigs, if desired. Serve immediately. Pass grated parmesan or romano cheese, if desired. Makes 6 to 8 servings.

1 Cover rice mixture with a tight-fitting lid. Simmer for 15 minutes (do not lift cover). Remove from heat. At this stage, the grains of rice will still have a hard core and not all of the liquid will be absorbed.

2 Stir tomato and snipped parsley into rice mixture. Cover and let stand for 5 to 8 minutes. The rice should be tender but still slightly firm, and the mixture should be creamy, as shown. If necessary, stir in a little Chicken Stock or water to reach the desired consistency.

Flavored Butters

Use flavored butters to spark up plain vegetables, meats, and breads. And let decorative butters add interest to any dinner menu—

To flavor ½ cup *butter or margarine*, soften it, then stir in the seasonings listed below for the desired flavor. To soften, cut the butter into pieces; place in heat-proof bowl in cool oven. Turn oven to 350°; heat 3 minutes. Transfer butter to cool bowl so it won't melt.

Honey Butter: Stir in ¼ cup *honey* and ½ teaspoon grated *lemon peel*. Serve with bread.

Orange Butter: Stir in 1 tablespoon *powdered sugar* and ½ teaspoon grated *orange peel*. Serve with bread.

Parsley Butter: Stir in 1 tablespoon snipped *parsley*; 1 teaspoon *lemon juice*; ¼ teaspoon dried *savory*, crushed; ⅛ teaspoon *salt*; and dash *pepper*. Serve with potatoes or bread.

Garlic Butter: Stir in 2 or 3 cloves *garlic*, minced. Spread on French bread slices before heating or spoon atop broiled steaks.

Herb Butter: Stir in ½ teaspoon dried *thyme*, crushed, and ½ teaspoon ground *sage*. Serve with vegetables or meat.

Tarragon Butter: Stir in 2 teaspoons *lemon juice* and 1 teaspoon dried *tarragon*, crushed. Serve with fish, beef, chicken, or vegetables.

Mustard Butter: Stir in ¼ cup *prepared mustard* and 2 tablespoons snipped *parsley*. Serve with beef, corned beef, or pork.

Blue Cheese Butter: Stir in ¼ cup crumbled *blue cheese*. Serve with baked potatoes.

Decorative Butters

Butter balls are easy to make if you have two butter paddles. Scald the paddles in boiling water, then chill in ice water. Cut cold, firm butter or margarine into ½-inch pats and form into a ball with fingers. Put butter on scored side of paddle. Hold bottom paddle still and move top paddle in circular motion (step 1). Chill butter balls in ice water. For individual pots of butter, use any small dishes or specially shaped butter dishes. Fill to the brim with softened butter or margarine and level with a knife. Then use a knife to make crisscross markings across the top (step 2). Chill; let stand at room temperature about 30 minutes before serving.

1 Hold the bottom paddle still; move top paddle in a circular motion, applying light pressure. If butter clings to paddles, scald and chill the paddles again. Place butter balls in ice water to chill.

2 Make crisscross or any decorative markings on top with a knife. Chill; let stand at room temperature about 30 minutes before serving so butter will spread easily. Top with parsley, if desired.

Kinds of Butter

Sweet cream butter, which is most common, is made from sweet cream and usually is lightly salted. Unsalted butter is also available. This butter is generally referred to as sweet butter and can be found in the frozen food counter at the grocery store. Whipped butter is butter that has air or other gases whipped into it, making it easier to spead. Since part of its volume is air, it cannot be directly substituted for regular butter for most uses.

Desserts

Nothing says "gourmet" quite like a luscious dessert. These irresistible treats include layered *English Trifle* (see recipe, page 82), a *Cream Puff* and *Eclair* filled with *Crème Pâtissière* (see recipes, page 83), lacy *Brandy Snaps* (see recipe, page 77), an individual *Candied Lemon Tart* (see recipe, page 88), *Poached Nectarines* in a raspberry sauce (see recipe, page 76), and refreshing *Strawberry Sorbet* (see recipe, page 86).

Chocolate Mousse

¼ cup sugar
1 envelope unflavored gelatin
1½ cups milk
4 squares (4 ounces) semisweet chocolate, cut up
4 beaten egg yolks
¼ cup rum
1 teaspoon vanilla
4 egg whites
2 tablespoons sugar
1 cup whipping cream
1 square (1 ounce) semisweet chocolate, grated
¼ cup currant jelly

For collar, fold a 23x9-inch piece of waxed paper lengthwise into thirds. Butter one side of the paper. Attach paper, buttered side in, around the top of a 1-quart soufflé dish so that paper extends 2 inches above dish (step 1).

In saucepan combine the ¼ cup sugar and gelatin. Stir in milk; add cut-up chocolate. Cook and stir over low heat till chocolate melts. Gradually stir about *half* of the hot mixture into egg yolks; return to remaining hot mixture in saucepan. Cook and stir for 2 to 3 minutes or till slightly thickened. *Do not boil.* Remove from heat; stir in rum and vanilla. Chill gelatin mixture to the consistency of corn syrup, stirring occasionally.

Immediately beat egg whites till soft peaks form. Gradually add the 2 tablespoons sugar, beating till stiff peaks form. When gelatin is partially set to the consistency of unbeaten egg whites (step 2), fold in stiff-beaten egg whites. Beat ½ *cup* of the whipping cream till soft peaks form. Fold whipped cream into gelatin mixture. Turn into prepared soufflé dish; chill till firm.

At serving time remove the collar. Press grated chocolate around the edge of the mousse (step 3). Beat remaining whipping cream; dollop atop. (If desired, pipe whipped cream through a pastry bag fitted with a flower tip.) Heat currant jelly; drizzle over mousse. Makes 6 to 8 servings.

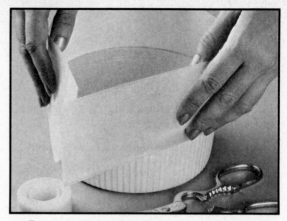

1 To attach collar, position the paper, buttered side in, around the top of the soufflé dish. Allow the paper to extend 2 inches above the dish. Secure with tape or a piece of string.

2 Place the gelatin mixture in the refrigerator to chill. Or, set the saucepan in a bowl of ice water for faster cooling, stirring frequently. When gelatin is the consistency of unbeaten egg whites, as shown, fold in egg whites.

3 To garnish the chilled mousse, press fine particles of grated chocolate around the top edge. Dollop or pipe on whipped cream; drizzle with melted jelly.

Crêpes Suzette

1 To spread crepe batter in skillet, rotate pan so batter flows evenly over bottom to form a thin, smooth layer. If the batter is too thick and won't flow, thin it by blending in a little milk.

Freeze extra crepes for another use. Stack alternately with waxed paper and place in a moisture-vaporproof bag. Thaw at room temperature. If desired, all ingredients can be doubled to make 8 servings. Pictured on the cover —

8 Dessert Crepes
¼ cup butter *or* margarine
¼ cup orange liqueur
¼ cup orange juice
3 tablespoons sugar
2 tablespoons brandy

Prepare Dessert Crepes. Fold each crepe in half, browned side out; fold crepe in half again, forming a triangle. For sauce, in chafing dish or skillet combine butter or margarine, orange liqueur, orange juice, and sugar; cook and stir till mixture is bubbly.

Arrange folded crepes in sauce in chafing dish or skillet. Simmer till sauce thickens slightly, spooning sauce over crepes as they heat. In small saucepan heat the brandy over low heat just till hot. Ignite; pour flaming brandy over crepes and sauce (step 3). Serves 4.

Dessert Crepes: Combine 1 cup all-purpose *flour*, 1½ cups *milk*, 2 *eggs*, 2 tablespoons *sugar*, 1 tablespoon *cooking oil*, and ⅛ teaspoon *salt*; beat with a rotary beater till blended. Heat a lightly greased 6-inch skillet. Remove from heat. Spoon in 2 tablespoons batter; lift and tilt skillet to spread batter (step 1). Return to heat; brown on one side. Loosen edge of crepe with small spatula. Invert pan over paper toweling; remove crepe (step 2). Repeat to make 16 to 18 crepes, greasing skillet as needed.

2 Remove crepe from pan by inverting over paper toweling and letting crepe fall; smooth if necessary so that crepe lies flat to cool.

Hints on Flaming

Although any liquor or liqueur will flame, for best results, choose a recently opened bottle that is at least 70 proof. One of this type will be easier to flame and will burn more brightly.

3 Heat the brandy in a small saucepan over low heat till it starts to vaporize. Using a long match, ignite the brandy. Pour the flaming brandy over the warm crepes and sauce.

Poached Nectarines

Choose ripe nectarines that are firm, yet slightly soft at the "seam." Rearrange the fruit occasionally during poaching to ensure an even doneness. Pictured on pages 72 and 73—

1½ **cups sugar**
1 **tablespoon lemon juice**
6 **medium nectarines *or* peaches**
1½ **cups fresh *or* frozen red raspberries**
3 **tablespoons orange liqueur**

In a 10-inch skillet combine sugar, lemon juice, and 1½ cups *water*. Bring to boiling. Meanwhile, halve nectarines or peaches lengthwise; remove and discard pits. Add nectarine or peach halves to skillet. Reduce heat; simmer, covered, for 5 to 10 minutes or till tender, stirring occasionally. Remove fruit and reserve ⅓ cup of the cooking liquid. Remove skin from fruit (step 1); keep fruit warm. Thaw raspberries, if frozen. Reserve a few raspberries for garnish. Press remaining raspberries through a sieve to remove seeds (step 2); discard seeds. To make raspberry sauce, in saucepan combine the raspberry pulp and juice, reserved cooking liquid, and orange liqueur; heat through. Arrange 2 nectarine or peach halves in each of 6 individual dessert dishes. Spoon warm sauce over fruit. Garnish with the reserved whole raspberries. Serve immediately. Serves 6.

About Fruit Varieties

There are two varieties of nectarines and peaches. If the pit clings to the flesh of the fruit and is difficult to remove, the fruit is of the "clingstone" variety. The "freestone" variety has easy-to-remove pits. Either type may have yellow or white flesh.

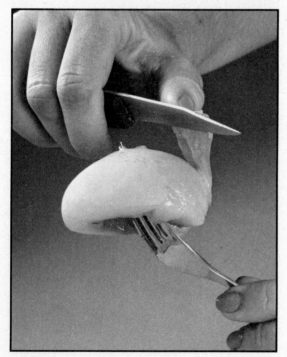

1 *To remove skins from nectarine or peach halves, hold fruit with a fork inserted into the cut side. Using a small paring knife, grasp skin at the edge and peel off in strips.*

2 *Use the back of a wooden spoon to press raspberries through a sieve to remove seeds. The seeds should remain in the sieve after the pulp and juice of the raspberries have passed through.*

Brandy Snaps

Shape these lacy cookies into cones while still warm. When cool, fill with brandy-flavored whipped cream. Pictured on pages 72 and 73—

- ½ **cup packed brown sugar**
- 6 **tablespoons butter** *or* **margarine, melted**
- ¼ **cup light molasses**
- 1 **tablespoon brandy**
- ¾ **cup all-purpose flour**
- ½ **teaspoon ground ginger**
- ½ **teaspoon ground nutmeg**
- ⅛ **teaspoon salt**
- 1 **cup whipping cream**
- 2 **tablespoons powdered sugar**
- 1 **tablespoon brandy**
  Grated chocolate *or* **ground nutmeg (optional)**

In mixing bowl combine brown sugar, butter, molasses, and 1 tablespoon brandy; mix well.

Stir together flour, ginger, ½ teaspoon nutmeg, and salt; stir into butter mixture. Drop batter by level tablespoonfuls 5 inches apart onto lightly greased cookie sheet. (Bake only 3 at a time; batter will spread to circles 4 to 5 inches in diameter.) Bake in 350° oven for 6 to 7 minutes. Let cool about 2 minutes on cookie sheet. Remove one at a time *while still warm* with a wide metal spatula and immediately shape into a cone (step 1). (If cookies cool and become hard before they are shaped, reheat in oven for 30 seconds.) Place cookies, seam-side down, on wire rack; cool. Store in airtight container.

Just before serving, beat whipping cream, powdered sugar, and 1 tablespoon brandy on high speed of electric mixer just till stiff peaks form. Spoon into pastry bag with star tip. Pipe whipped cream into each Brandy Snap (step 2). Sprinkle whipped cream with grated chocolate or nutmeg. Serve immediately. Makes 20.

1 Shape warm cookies into cones by turning opposite sides of cookie in toward center. Sides should overlap to form a point at one end and a wide opening at the other end.

2 Prop the cooled cone-shaped cookie upright in a small glass for easier handling. Using a pastry bag with a star tip, fill each cookie with the sweetened, brandy-flavored whipped cream.

Baklava

(BOCK-luh-vah)

Allowing this pastry to stand overnight gives the flavors time to blend and makes it easier to eat—

16 ounces frozen filo dough
    (21 16x12-inch sheets)
4 cups finely chopped walnuts
3 cups finely chopped pecans
¾ cup sugar
1 tablespoon ground cinnamon
1½ cups *unsalted* butter, melted
2 cups sugar
1 cup water
2 tablespoons honey
2 tablespoons lemon juice
4 inches stick cinnamon

Thaw frozen filo dough at room temperature for 2 hours. Cut the 16x12-inch sheets in half crosswise. (If filo is a different size, cut to fit pan.) Cover with a slightly damp towel. Lightly butter the bottom of a 13x9x2-inch baking pan. Combine the walnuts, pecans, the ¾ cup sugar, and ground cinnamon; set aside.

Layer *nine* of the half-sheets of filo in the pan, brushing each sheet with some of the melted butter. Sprinkle about *1 cup* of the nut mixture over the filo in the pan. Drizzle with some of the melted butter. Top with another *four* half-sheets of the filo, brushing each with more of the melted butter (step 1). Repeat the nut and 4-half-sheet filo layers *five* times more. Sprinkle with the remaining nut mixture. Drizzle with some of the melted butter. Top with the remaining *nine* half-sheets of filo, brushing each with some of the remaining melted butter. Cut into diamond-shaped pieces or squares, cutting to *but not through* the bottom layer (step 2). Bake in 325° oven for 60 minutes. Finish cutting diamonds or squares; cool thoroughly on wire rack.

Meanwhile, in a saucepan combine the 2 cups sugar, the water, honey, lemon juice, and stick cinnamon. Boil gently, uncovered, for 15 minutes. Remove from heat. Remove cinnamon. Stir till blended. Pour warm syrup over cooled pastry. Cool completely. Garnish each diamond with a whole clove, if desired. Makes 3 to 4 dozen pieces.

1 *Top the nut mixture with sheets of filo, brushing the top side of each sheet with melted butter after it has been placed in the pan.*

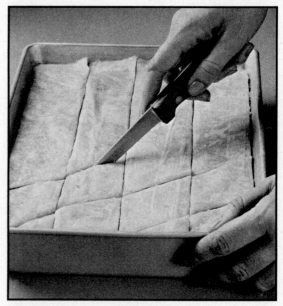

2 *Before baking, cut Baklava with a sharp knife into diamond-shaped pieces or squares, cutting to but not through the bottom layer. After baking, finish cutting the pieces.*

Coffee Custard

A baked custard with a caramel coating—

1¼ teaspoons instant coffee crystals
⅓ cup hot water
4 eggs
1 cup milk
⅔ cup light cream
⅓ cup sugar
½ teaspoon vanilla
⅓ cup sugar
Whipped cream
Chocolate curls

Dissolve coffee crystals in hot water. In medium bowl lightly beat the eggs. Stir in the coffee mixture, milk, light cream, ⅓ cup sugar, and vanilla. Set aside.

In heavy skillet heat the remaining ⅓ cup sugar over low heat without stirring till it starts to melt. Continue heating, stirring constantly, about 10 minutes or till golden brown (step 1); remove from heat. Immediately pour into a 3-cup metal ring mold; quickly swirl to cover bottom and sides (step 2). Set mold in a 9x9x2-inch baking pan on oven rack. Pour egg mixture into mold. Pour hot water around mold to depth of 1 inch. Bake in 325° oven about 45 minutes or till knife inserted near center of custard comes out clean. Chill 2 to 3 hours. To unmold chilled custard, first loosen edge with knife or spatula; slip point of knife down the side to let in air. Invert onto serving platter. Garnish center with whipped cream and chocolate curls. Makes 6 servings.

Baked Custards

The success of a baked custard depends on the ratio of eggs to milk. As a general rule, one egg per half-cup milk produces a soft baked custard that holds its shape as gelatin does. Turn a basic baked custard into anything from an appetizer to a dessert simply by adding other ingredients. Quiche, strata, and pumpkin pie are actually baked custard variations.

1 Heat the sugar in a heavy skillet without stirring till it starts to melt. As the sugar is heated, it will turn golden brown. Heat and stir about 10 minutes more or till golden brown. This step is called caramelizing.

2 Immediately pour the caramelized sugar into a 3-cup metal ring mold. Swirl to cover bottom and sides. Work quickly to coat the mold before the sugar hardens.

Puff Pastry

Fill Patty Shells with a meat, poultry, or seafood mixture to serve as a main course—

- **1 cup butter *or* margarine, chilled**
- **1¾ cups all-purpose flour**
- **½ cup ice water**

Reserve *2 tablespoons* of the butter or margarine; keep chilled. In mixing bowl work the remaining chilled butter or margarine with the back of a spoon just till pliable. Pat or roll out butter between two sheets of waxed paper into an 8x6-inch rectangle. Chill butter at least 1 hour in refrigerator or 20 minutes in freezer.

Cut reserved 2 tablespoons butter into flour till mixture resembles coarse crumbs. Gradually add ice water; toss with fork. Shape into a ball. Knead on floured surface till smooth (about 5 minutes). Cover; let rest 10 minutes.

On lightly floured surface, roll out dough into a 15x9-inch rectangle. Place chilled butter on half of the dough. Fold over other half to cover butter; seal edges of dough (step 1). Wrap in waxed paper; chill at least 1 hour in refrigerator. On lightly floured surface, roll out dough into a 15x9-inch rectangle, rolling from center just to edges. Brush off any excess flour. Gently lift dough, without stretching, and fold into thirds. Turn dough; fold into thirds again. Press edges to seal. Wrap in waxed paper; chill at least 1 hour in refrigerator. Repeat rolling, folding, and chilling dough 2 or 3 more times. Prepare Patty Shells, Napoleons, or Puff Pastry Twists.

Patty Shells

On lightly floured surface, roll out dough into a 14x10-inch rectangle. With a 3½-inch round cutter, cut dough into circles. (If desired, cut dough with a scalloped round cutter.) Using a 2½-inch round cutter, make a cut in the center of each 3½-inch circle but *do not cut through dough* (step 2). Place circles on a baking sheet covered with 3 or 4 thicknesses of white paper toweling. (Do not reroll pastry trimmings.) Chill.

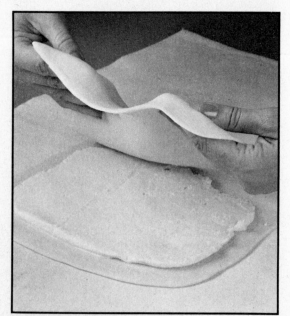

1 *Place chilled butter on half the dough. Carefully lift other half and lay over butter to cover. With heel of hand, seal all 3 edges. Sealing the butter between layers of dough contributes to the flaky quality of the baked pastry.*

2 *For Patty Shells, position a 2½-inch round cutter over a 3½-inch circle of dough. Press down just enough to cut through the top surface of the dough. This cut defines the center portion, which is later removed for the filling.*

Bake on towel-lined baking sheet in 450° oven for 5 minutes. Reduce oven temperature to 300°. Continue baking for 20 to 25 minutes or till pastry is lightly browned. Remove the center portion with a fork. Return pastry to oven; bake 5 minutes more. Remove; cool on wire rack. To serve, fill with sweetened whipped cream, Crème Pâtissière (see recipe, page 83), ice cream, or a cream pudding. Makes 8 to 10.

Napoleons

On lightly floured surface, roll out dough into a 14x8-inch rectangle. Trim edges; prick dough well with a fork. With a sharp knife cut dough into sixteen 3½x2-inch rectangles. Place on a baking sheet that is covered with 3 or 4 thicknesses of white paper toweling. Chill well.

Combine 1 slightly beaten *egg white* and 1 tablespoon *ice water*; brush over dough. Bake on towel-lined baking sheet in 450° oven for 6 minutes. Reduce oven temperature to 300°.

Continue baking for 20 to 25 minutes or till pastry is lightly browned and crisp. Remove; cool.

To serve, separate each pastry into 3 layers (step 3). Spread Crème Pâtissière between layers of pastry; glaze top with Chocolate Icing (see recipes, page 83). Makes 16 Napoleons.

Puff Pastry Twists

On lightly floured surface, roll out dough into a 14x10-inch rectangle. Brush 1 beaten *egg* over surface of the dough; sprinkle with ½ cup finely chopped *toasted almonds*. With a sharp knife cut dough lengthwise into two 14x5-inch rectangles. Cut crosswise into 5x½-inch strips (step 4). Twist each strip of dough; place 1 inch apart on a baking sheet that is covered with 3 or 4 thicknesses of white paper toweling. Chill.

Bake on towel-lined baking sheet in 450° oven 5 minutes. Reduce temperature to 300°. Continue baking 10 to 15 minutes. Sift *powdered sugar* over pastries. Makes 56.

3 For Napoleons, separate each cooled baked pastry into 3 layers with a fork, as shown. Work carefully to avoid breaking the light, flaky pastry. Spread Crème Pâtissière between each layer. Glaze the top with Chocolate Icing.

4 For Puff Pastry Twists, cut dough lengthwise into two 14x5-inch rectangles. Using a ruler as a guide, cut each rectangle crosswise into strips 5 inches long and ½ inch wide. Twist each strip; place on prepared pan.

English Trifle

This classic dessert—cake cubes sprinkled with sherry, spread with jelly and fruit, and topped with custard and whipped cream — is pictured on pages 72 and 73. Serve English Trifle in a clear glass bowl to display the layers—

2 recipes Sponge Cake (see recipe, page 85)
2 eggs
1 egg yolk
1¾ cups light cream
¼ cup granulated sugar
½ cup cream sherry
½ cup currant jelly
2 medium peaches, peeled, pitted, and sliced*
1 cup sliced fresh strawberries*
½ cup whipping cream
1 tablespoon powdered sugar
¼ teaspoon vanilla

Prepare Sponge Cake in two 8x1½-inch round cake pans. Cool cake layers. Cut into ½-inch cubes (should have about 9 cups). For custard, in heavy saucepan beat eggs and egg yolk. Stir in light cream and granulated sugar. Cook and stir over medium heat till mixture coats a metal spoon (step 1). Pour custard into a medium bowl; set inside a larger bowl filled with ice. Stir occasionally.

Place *half* of the cake cubes in bottom of a 2- to 2½-quart clear glass bowl. Sprinkle cake with some of the cream sherry; dollop with currant jelly. Spoon peaches and strawberries over. Top with the remaining cake cubes; sprinkle with the remaining sherry. Spoon cooled custard over cake (step 2).

Beat whipping cream, powdered sugar, and vanilla till soft peaks form. Spoon whipped cream over custard. Cover and refrigerate at least 6 hours or overnight. Before serving, garnish with additional fresh fruit and a mint sprig, if desired. Makes 12 servings.

*If desired, substitute 2 cups frozen *mixed fruit,* thawed and drained, for the fresh peaches and strawberries. Garnish with toasted slivered *almonds* instead of the fresh fruit.

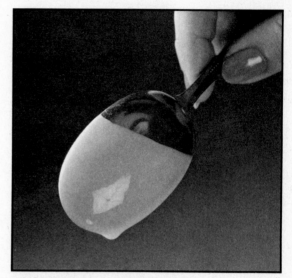

1 Cook custard mixture till it starts to thicken and coats a metal spoon. Dip the spoon into the custard mixture; it should drip off, leaving a coating slightly thicker than milk. The coating should hold its shape when you wipe a finger across the spoon. Use a clean spoon for each test.

2 Cool custard in a bowl set in ice. Pouring the custard out of the saucepan speeds cooling and helps prevent curdling. Spoon the cooled custard over the top layer of moistened cake cubes.

Cream Puffs

Delicate Cream Puffs and Eclairs are pictured on pages 72 and 73. Make both pastries from the same dough. If you like, fill them with sweetened whipped cream, ice cream, or cream pudding instead of Crème Pâtissière—

½ **cup butter** *or* **margarine**
1 **cup all-purpose flour**
¼ **teaspoon salt**
4 **eggs**
  Crème Pâtissière
  Chocolate Icing *or* **powdered sugar (optional)**

In medium saucepan melt butter. Add 1 cup *water;* bring to boiling. Add flour and salt all at once; stir vigorously. Cook and stir till mixture forms a ball that doesn't separate (step 1). Remove from heat; cool about 10 minutes. Add eggs, one at a time, beating with a wooden spoon about 30 seconds after each addition.

For large puffs, drop dough by heaping tablespoonfuls 3 inches apart onto greased baking sheet (step 2). Bake in 400° oven about 30 minutes or till golden brown and puffy. For small puffs, drop by heaping teaspoonfuls 2 inches apart onto greased baking sheet. Bake in 400° oven about 20 minutes. Split large and small puffs; remove any soft dough (step 3).

Cool on wire rack. Fill with Crème Pâtissière. Glaze with Chocolate Icing or sprinkle with powdered sugar, if desired. Makes about 10 large or 60 small Cream Puffs.

Crème Pâtissière: In heavy saucepan combine ⅔ cup *sugar,* 2 tablespoons *cornstarch,* and ¼ teaspoon *salt.* Stir in 2 cups *milk.* Cook and stir till thickened and bubbly. Remove from heat. Stir about *half* of the hot mixture into 3 beaten *egg yolks;* return to remaining mixture. Bring to boiling; cook and stir 2 minutes longer. Stir in 1 tablespoon *butter* and 1 teaspoon *vanilla.* Cover surface with clear plastic wrap; cool.

Chocolate Icing: Melt 2 ounces *sweet cooking chocolate* and 2 tablespoons *butter.* Remove from heat. Stir in 1 cup sifted *powdered sugar* and enough *hot water* (2 to 3 tablespoons) to make of glazing consistency. Cool.

Eclairs

Prepare Cream Puff dough as above. Spoon dough into a pastry bag with a 1- to 1¼-inch opening. Pipe dough onto greased baking sheet. Make Eclairs about 5 inches long and 1½ to 1¾ inches wide. Bake in 400° oven about 30 minutes. Split, cool, and fill as for Cream Puffs. Makes 8.

1 Once the flour and salt are added, cook mixture over medium heat, stirring constantly, till it forms a smooth ball that doesn't separate. Remove from heat; cool about 10 minutes.

2 For large puffs, drop dough by heaping tablespoonfuls 3 inches apart onto greased baking sheet. Use a spatula to push the dough off spoon. Shape dough into even mounds.

3 To prevent Cream Puffs from collapsing when removed from oven, immediately split each puff. The puff may have a slightly soft center. This soft dough may be lifted out.

Almond Torte

½ cup butter *or* margarine
6 slightly beaten eggs
1 cup granulated sugar
1 cup all-purpose flour
½ teaspoon vanilla
½ teaspoon almond extract
  Almond Filling
9 tablespoons strawberry jam
½ cup whipping cream
1 tablespoon powdered sugar
1 tablespoon light rum

Melt butter; cool. In top of double boiler combine eggs and granulated sugar. Set over hot but not boiling water (water in bottom of double boiler should not touch top pan). Stir over low heat about 10 minutes or till lukewarm. Pour into large mixer bowl. Beat at high speed of electric mixer about 15 minutes or till light and tripled in volume (step 1). Gently fold in flour, ⅓ at a time. Fold in butter, vanilla, and almond extract. Pour into 2 greased and lightly floured 8x1½-inch round cake pans. Bake in 350° oven for 25 to 30 minutes or till done. Cool in pans 10 minutes; remove and cool on wire racks.

Split each cake layer in half horizontally (step 2). To assemble, spread one cake slice with ⅓ of the Almond Filling, then with *3 tablespoons* of the jam. Repeat layers of cake, filling, and jam 2 more times (step 3). Top with final cake slice. Beat together whipping cream, powdered sugar, and rum till soft peaks form; spread over top of cake. Garnish with halved fresh strawberries, if desired. Serves 10 to 12.

Almond Filling: Crumble *Homemade Almond Paste* (see tip, below) *or* one 8-ounce can *almond paste.* Add 6 tablespoons softened *butter;* cream. Add ¼ cup *light rum;* beat till smooth.

Homemade Almond Paste

Place 1 cup *blanched whole almonds* on baking sheet. Heat in 300° oven 10 minutes; do not brown. Remove and cool.

Place steel blade in work bowl of food processor; add almonds. Process about 1 minute or till ground. Add 1⅓ cups sifted *powdered sugar* and 2 tablespoons *water.* If desired, add ½ teaspoon *almond extract.* Process about 15 seconds or till mixture forms a ball.

1 Beat egg mixture at high speed of electric mixer about 15 minutes or till light. Lift the beaters and check consistency, as shown. The egg mixture should triple in volume.

2 Split each cake layer in half horizontally. As a cutting guide, insert wooden picks halfway up the side of cake layer. Then use a serrated, long-bladed knife to slice through the layer.

3 Place one cake slice on serving platter. Spread with ⅓ of the Almond Filling, then 3 tablespoons jam. Repeat layers 2 more times. Top with remaining cake slice.

Baked Alaska

Visit an ice cream specialty shop to choose your favorite ice cream for this impressive dessert—

Sponge Cake
1 **quart ice cream**
4 **egg whites**
1 **teaspoon vanilla**
½ **teaspoon cream of tartar**
⅔ **cup sugar**
¼ **cup chopped walnuts**

Prepare Sponge Cake. In a 1½-quart freezer-proof bowl stir the ice cream with a wooden spoon to soften. Press the ice cream evenly into the bowl, leveling the surface (step 1). Cover and return ice cream to freezer till firm.

Place cake on a freezer-to-oven serving platter.* Loosen the ice cream from the bowl with a spatula. Invert ice cream onto Sponge Cake, centering the ice cream over the cake layer (step 2). Cover; freeze till firm.

At serving time beat egg whites, vanilla, and cream of tartar till soft peaks form. Gradually add sugar, beating till stiff peaks form. Fold in nuts. Spread frozen cake and ice cream with egg white mixture, sealing to edge of cake and platter all around (step 3). Swirl in a circular motion to make decorative peaks. Bake in 500° oven about 3 minutes or till golden. Cut into wedges and serve immediately. Serves 8.

*If you do not have a freezer-to-oven serving platter, loosely wrap cake with ice cream in foil and freeze till firm. At serving time transfer cake and ice cream to baking sheet. Spread with egg white mixture; bake as directed.

Sponge Cake: In mixer bowl beat 1 *egg* at high speed of electric mixer about 4 minutes or till thick and lemon-colored. Gradually add ½ cup *sugar;* continue beating at medium speed for 4 to 5 minutes or till sugar dissolves.

Stir together ½ cup all-purpose *flour,* ½ teaspoon *baking powder,* and ⅛ teaspoon *salt.* Add flour mixture to egg mixture; stir just till blended. In small saucepan heat ¼ cup *milk* and 1 tablespoon *butter* till butter melts; stir into batter and mix well. Turn into a greased 8x1½-inch round cake pan. Bake in 350° oven about 20 minutes or till cake springs back and leaves no imprint when lightly touched. Cool on wire rack 10 minutes. Remove from pan.

1 Use your favorite flavor of ice cream. Soften ice cream just till pliable. Press ice cream into bottom of bowl with a rubber spatula. Smooth surface so ice cream will rest evenly on cake.

2 Place freezer-to-oven serving platter on a piece of foil; place Sponge Cake on platter. Carefully invert ice cream onto cake, centering it over the cake layer. Bring foil up and over cake and ice cream, covering lightly. Freeze till firm.

3 Using a narrow metal spatula, spread egg white mixture over ice cream and cake. Spread to edge of cake and platter, sealing all around. Swirl to make peaks.

Cherry Sorbet

The strawberry variation is pictured on pages 72 and 73—

- **2 cups fresh *or* frozen pitted dark sweet cherries**
- **1 cup water**
- **½ cup sugar**
- **½ cup light cream**
- **¼ cup lemon juice**
- **2 egg whites**
- **¼ cup sugar**

Thaw cherries, if frozen. In saucepan combine water, the ½ cup sugar, and dash *salt*. Bring to boiling; reduce heat. Simmer 5 minutes; cool. In blender container or food processor bowl combine cherries and cream. Cover; blend till smooth (about 1 minute). Stir in cooled sugar syrup and lemon juice. Turn into a 9x9x2-inch pan; cover and freeze till firm.

Beat egg whites till soft peaks form; gradually add the ¼ cup sugar, beating till stiff peaks form. Break the frozen mixture into chunks (step 1); turn into chilled mixer bowl. Beat smooth with electric mixer (step 2). Fold in beaten egg whites. Return to cold pan; cover and freeze till firm. Let stand at room temperature for 5 minutes before serving. Scoop to serve (step 3). Makes 6 to 8 servings.

Peach-Orange Sorbet

Prepare Cherry Sorbet as above *except* substitute 2 or 3 *peaches*, peeled, pitted, and chopped (should have about 2 cups), for the cherries, and ¼ cup *orange juice* for the lemon juice. Stir 1 tablespoon finely shredded *orange peel* into the fruit and cream mixture in blender or food processor.

Pineapple Sorbet

Prepare Cherry Sorbet as above *except* substitute one 8-ounce can *crushed pineapple* (juice pack) for the cherries, and ¼ cup *orange juice* for the lemon juice.

Strawberry Sorbet

Prepare Cherry Sorbet as above *except* substitute 2 cups fresh *or* frozen whole *strawberries* for the cherries.

Watermelon Sorbet

Prepare Cherry Sorbet as above *except* substitute 2 cups cubed *watermelon* for the cherries, and decrease the lemon juice to *3 tablespoons*.

1 Break the frozen cherry mixture into chunks with a wooden spoon. The chunks should be small enough for easy mixing with an electric mixer or rotary beater. Transfer the broken-up mixture to a large chilled mixer bowl.

2 Beat the mixture to break up large chunks. Continue breaking till smooth; do not allow to melt. Scrape down sides of bowl as needed. This beating helps form small ice crystals, incorporates air, and increases volume.

3 Let sorbet stand at room temperature for 5 minutes before serving. This makes scooping easier with an ice cream scoop. If desired, garnish individual servings with a fresh fruit that complements the sorbet.

Baumkuchen
(Bowm-KYOO-Kin)

Use a standard mixer to beat the eggs —

- **10 egg yolks**
- **¾ cup butter** *or* **margarine, softened**
- **¾ cup sugar**
- **2 teaspoons finely shredded lemon peel**
- **1 teaspoon vanilla**
- **1 cup all-purpose flour**
- **½ cup cornstarch**
- **10 egg whites**
- **¼ cup sugar**
  Vanilla Glaze
  Chocolate Glaze

In mixer bowl beat egg yolks at high speed of electric mixer about 10 minutes or till thick and lemon-colored. In large mixer bowl beat butter about 30 seconds; gradually add the ¾ cup sugar, lemon peel, and vanilla. Add egg yolks, beating well. Stir together flour, cornstarch, and ¼ teaspoon *salt;* stir in butter mixture. Wash beaters and the large mixer bowl thoroughly. In large mixer bowl beat egg whites till soft peaks form. Gradually add the ¼ cup sugar, beating till stiff peaks form. Fold into flour mixture.

Grease an 8-inch springform pan; spread ⅓ *cup* batter evenly in the bottom. Place under broiler 5 inches from heat; broil about 1 minute or till lightly browned. (Give pan a half-turn for even browning, if needed.) Do not overbrown. Remove from broiler. Spread another ⅓ cup batter atop first layer (step 1). Broil as before, turning, if necessary. Repeat, making 15 to 17 layers in all. Cool 10 minutes. Loosen cake and remove sides of pan; cool completely. Cut into 12 wedges. Place wedges on wire rack with waxed paper beneath. Spread Vanilla Glaze over *half* the wedges (step 2); spread Chocolate Glaze over remainder. Let dry. Serves 12.

Vanilla Glaze: Combine 2 cups sifted *powdered sugar* and 1 teaspoon *vanilla.* Add enough *milk* (about 2 tablespoons) to make of spooning consistency.

Chocolate Glaze: Melt 1½ squares (1½ ounces) *unsweetened chocolate* and 2 tablespoons *butter or margarine* over low heat, stirring constantly; remove from heat. Stir in 1½ cups sifted *powdered sugar* and 1 teaspoon *vanilla* till crumbly. Add enough *boiling water* (about 2 tablespoons) to make of spooning consistency.

1 After broiling first layer of batter, spread ⅓ cup batter evenly over the cooked layer. Broil till lightly browned, turning the pan if necessary for even browning. Continue spreading batter and broiling to make a total of 15 to 17 layers.

2 Cut cooled cake into 12 wedges. Place on wire rack so pieces don't touch each other. Place rack over sheet of waxed paper. Spoon glaze over wedges and spread evenly, as shown. Tilt wedges slightly and spoon icing onto sides of each piece. Let dry thoroughly.

Candied Lemon Tarts

Candied lemon slices accent these attractive glazed tarts. Pictured on pages 72 and 73—

- **1 lemon**
  Pastry for Single-Crust Pie
- **1 cup sugar**
- **3 tablespoons cornstarch**
- **2 beaten egg yolks**
- **2 tablespoons butter or margarine**
- **¼ teaspoon finely shredded lemon peel**
- **2 tablespoons lemon juice**
- **¼ cup sugar**
- **¼ teaspoon vanilla**

Slice lemon about ⅛ inch thick. Carefully remove seeds. Place lemon slices in a bowl; cover with *boiling water*. Let stand till cool. Drain and place in a small saucepan; cover with ¾ cup *cold water*. Bring to boiling; reduce heat. Simmer about 15 minutes or till lemon peel is soft. Remove from heat; cool.

Prepare and roll out pastry into a 13½x9-inch rectangle; cut into six 4½-inch squares. Fit over 6 inverted 6-ounce custard cups, pinching pleats at intervals to fit around cups (step 1). Prick bottoms; place inverted cups on baking sheet. (Or, line 6 tart pans with the pastry. Trim pastry and prick bottoms.) Bake in 475° oven for 8 to 10 minutes or till golden. Cool.

For filling, in saucepan combine 1 cup sugar, cornstarch, and dash *salt*. Gradually stir in 1 cup *water*. Cook and stir over medium-high heat till thickened and bubbly. Reduce heat; cook and stir 2 minutes more. Remove from heat. Stir about *half* of the hot mixture into beaten egg yolks; return to remaining hot mixture. Bring to a gentle boil. Cook and stir 2 minutes more. Remove from heat. Add butter and lemon peel. Gradually stir in lemon juice, mixing well. Spoon filling into cooled tart shells (step 2). Cool.

Meanwhile, drain lemon slices, reserving ¼ cup liquid. In saucepan combine reserved liquid and the ¼ cup sugar. Cook and stir over low heat till sugar is dissolved. Bring to boiling. Boil, uncovered, 12 minutes. Add lemon slices; simmer gently 5 minutes. Remove from heat. Arrange lemon slices over tarts. Stir vanilla into syrup. Spoon syrup over lemon slices (step 3). Cool; chill thoroughly. Serves 6.

Pastry for Single-Crust Pie: In mixing bowl stir together 1¼ cups all-purpose *flour* and ½ teaspoon *salt*. Cut in ⅓ cup *shortening* till pieces are the size of small peas. Using 3 to 4 tablespoons *cold water*, sprinkle 1 tablespoon water over part of the mixture; gently toss with a fork. Push to side of bowl. Repeat till all is moistened. Form dough into a ball.

1 Fit a square of dough over inverted custard cup. Pinch pleats at intervals so pastry will fit around cup. Or, fit dough into tart pan. Prick bottom of pastry to help prevent crust from puffing.

2 Gradually stir lemon juice into hot filling. The lemon juice is added last since acid can decrease the thickening power of cornstarch and curdle the egg. Spoon filling into shells.

3 Remove lemon slices from hot syrup and arrange over tarts. Stir vanilla into syrup. Spoon syrup over tarts, covering lemon slices and surface of filling. Cool; store in refrigerator.

Dessert Coffees

Complete a gourmet meal with a steaming cup of flavored coffee. Try the liqueur variations, and then experiment by adding a favorite liqueur to your coffee. Cappuccino, Turkish Coffee, and Coffee Milano are specialties you're sure to enjoy—

To ½ cup double-strength hot *coffee*, stir in the ingredients for the desired flavored coffee. Top with a dollop of sweetened *whipped cream*. Makes 1 serving.

Orange Coffee: Stir in 2 tablespoons *chocolate-flavored syrup* and 2 tablespoons *orange liqueur*. Garnish with an orange twist.

Coffee Benedictine: Stir in 2 tablespoons *Benedictine* and 2 tablespoons *light cream*. Sprinkle ground *nutmeg* over the whipped cream.

Cafe Mocha: Stir in 2 tablespoons *coffee liqueur* and 1 tablespoon *chocolate-flavored syrup*.

Chocolate-Mint Coffee: Stir in 2 tablespoons *chocolate-mint liqueur*. Garnish with chocolate curls or grated chocolate.

Irish Coffee: Stir in 1 tablespoon *Irish whiskey* and 2 teaspoons *sugar*.

Coffee Double: Stir in 1 tablespoon *coffee liqueur* and 1 tablespoon *brandy*.

Coffee Almond: Stir in 2 tablespoons *crème d' almond*.

Cappuccino

Combine ½ cup *whipping cream* and 1 tablespoon *powdered sugar*; beat till stiff peaks form. Pour 2 cups hot *espresso coffee* into 6 small cups, filling cups only half full. Add a large spoonful of whipped cream to each cup. Sprinkle each with finely shredded *orange peel*. If desired, sprinkle with ground *cinnamon* and ground *nutmeg*. Gently stir whipped cream into espresso coffee till melted. Makes 6 servings.

Note: For espresso coffee, use finely ground espresso roast coffee and brew in an ordinary coffeepot, *or* prepare instant espresso coffee powder according to package directions to make 2 cups.

For Turkish Coffee, bring the coffee mixture to boiling. As soon as the liquid foams, lift the saucepan away from the heat, as shown, and stir till the foaming subsides. Repeat boiling till foamy and removing from heat twice more. This cooking method gives Turkish Coffee its unique flavor.

Turkish Coffee

In large saucepan combine 6 cups *water* and ½ cup *sugar*; bring to boiling. Remove from heat; stir in ¾ cup ground *Turkish coffee*. Return to heat immediately. Bring to boiling again. As soon as the liquid foams, lift pan from heat and stir till foaming subsides (see photo). Repeat boiling and removing from heat 2 more times. Strain and serve immediately in demitasse cups. Makes 6 cups.

Coffee Milano

Place ½ cup regular-grind *coffee* in basket of coffee maker; sprinkle ¼ teaspoon ground *cinnamon* over top. Using 4 cups *water*, prepare coffee according to manufacturer's directions. Dip rims of 6 small brandy snifters in 1 slightly beaten *egg white*, then in *sugar*. Add 1 tablespoon *Galliano* and 2 teaspoons *coffee liqueur* to *each* snifter. Pour in ½ cup of the hot coffee. Top each with *whipped cream*. Serves 6.

Basic Techniques

Understanding basic cooking techniques is essential to preparing successful recipes — especially gourmet recipes. Here we've described several food and equipment techniques. When preparing the recipes in this book, use this section of helpful information to supplement the how-to photos that accompany each recipe. Mastering the basics makes gourmet cooking easy!

Egg whites beaten to soft peaks: *Egg whites should be placed in a deep, straight-sided glass or metal bowl. You can use a wire whisk, rotary beater, or electric mixer to beat air into the whites — just be sure beaters and bowl are clean and free of grease and egg yolk. Beat the egg whites till the tips of the peaks bend over in soft curls when the beaters are lifted. Adding cream of tartar or sugar helps stabilize the beaten whites.*

Egg whites beaten to stiff peaks: *After the soft-peak stage, egg whites reach the stiff-peak stage quickly. Continue beating till tips of peaks stand straight when beaters are lifted. The whites now contain all the air they can hold. Further beating makes them dry — and unsuitable for most purposes. Use stiff-beaten egg whites immediately; if left standing, they lose liquid and volume.*

Folding in egg whites: *Beaten egg whites should be folded into a mixture very gently, never stirred, so that the egg whites retain the air that was beaten into them. To make folding easier, lighten a thick batter by folding a small amount of beaten whites into the batter. Then fold that lightened batter back into the remaining whites. Use a rubber spatula and a circular down-up-and-over motion while turning the bowl.*

Thick and lemon-colored egg yolks: *Yolks that are beaten with an electric mixer turn a pale yellow and thicken to the point that they almost mound. When the beaters are lifted, the yolks flow in a thick stream. In baked foods, the beaten yolks act as a leavening agent, causing the product to rise as the incorporated air heats and expands. In uncooked foods such as a mousse, the yolks give a rich, airy texture.*

Garlic: *Mince or crush a garlic clove so that its strong flavor and aroma are evenly distributed throughout a food. The finer the pieces, the stronger the flavor. To crush garlic, place a peeled garlic clove in a garlic press, then clamp the handles together. Be sure to clean the press thoroughly after each use. Use a sharp utility knife to mince garlic, cutting it into very tiny, irregularly shaped pieces.*

Snipping fresh herbs: *Put the fresh herb in a container, such as a 1-cup glass measure, and snip with kitchen shears. To check the quantity needed for the recipe, use the proper measuring spoon. To substitute fresh herbs for dried, use three times more of the fresh herb. To freeze fresh herbs, wash and then blanch in boiling water for 10 seconds. Chill the herbs in ice water for 1 minute and pat dry. Wrap in foil, freeze.*

Whisks: Foods become frothy and smooth when beaten with a whisk. Most whisks are made of wire loops fastened to a handle, but some are made of wood. Whisks range in size from tiny ones, suitable for beating one egg, to large balloon-shaped whisks for beating doughs. A whisk is especially useful to prepare a smooth egg-thickened sauce, as shown. Also use this utensil to beat egg whites in a copper bowl.

Chef's knife: Any chopping job becomes easier with proper use of a chef's knife. The knife is designed with enough room to grasp the handle so that the fingers don't touch the chopping board while chopping. Grasp the handle firmly, and lightly place the fingers of the other hand on the tip of the blade. To efficiently chop, rock the knife handle up and down, keeping the tip of the knife on the cutting board.

Sharpening knives: Carving, slicing, and chopping are easier with a sharp knife. Sharpen knives with a sharpening steel or stone. With a sharpening steel in one hand, hold the knife at a 20-degree angle to the sharpener. Draw the blade edge over sharpener using an across-and-down motion. Turn blade over, reverse directions, and sharpen other side an equal number of times.

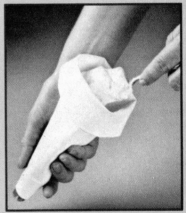

Whole Spices: Allspice, cinnamon, cloves, black pepper, and nutmeg are available in whole form. Whole spices are ideal for foods that cook slowly. To use whole spices, place them in a cheesecloth bag for easy removal. Grate whole nutmeg before using. A special nutmeg grater is available for this job, as shown. Use freshly grated nutmeg just as you would ground nutmeg.

Mortar and pestle: Dried herbs, aromatic seeds, garlic cloves, and nuts will release more of their flavor when crushed with a mortar and pestle. The mortar is a deep bowl in which the ingredients are placed. The tool used for crushing is the pestle. For a uniform grind, crush a small amount at a time. These tools also are useful for blending together several different seasonings.

Pastry bag: This flexible cone-shaped bag, often with a fancy tip, can be filled with frosting or whipped cream for decorating foods. The bag also can be filled with a soft dough to form various shapes for baking. Neatly fill the pastry bag by folding over the top of the bag about 1½ inches. Spoon the desired food into the bag, filling it only about two-thirds full. Unfold the top, twist closed, and squeeze to release contents.

Garnishes

Garnishes are important to every gourmet recipe, since good food always should be appealing to the eye as well as to the palate. Garnishes "frame" the food, providing a contrast of color and texture. They should be used simply and sparingly, and should never overpower the food. The suggestions given below will show you how to prepare simple garnishes that will add flair and appeal to your menus.

Frosted grapes: Cut grapes into small clusters of about 3 to 5 grapes each. Combine 1 slightly beaten egg white with a little water (about 2 teaspoons). Brush clusters of grapes with the egg white mixture. Sprinkle with sugar and place on a rack to dry.

Radish accordions: Trim roots and leaves from long narrow radishes. In each radish make about 8 to 10 narrow crosswise cuts about ⅛ inch wide, cutting partially through the radish (do not cut through the base). Place in ice water so slices will fan out.

Pepper flower: Using a sharp knife, make several lengthwise slashes through a 2- to 3-inch-long Serrano chili pepper to produce a fringe. Do not cut through stem; all pieces should remain attached. When placed in ice water, ends curl to resemble an opening flower.

Citrus cartwheels and twists: Slice lemons, limes, and oranges ⅛ inch thick. For cartwheels, cut V-shaped notches around the outside of the slice. For twists, cut halfway into center of the slice and twist ends in opposite directions. Give lemon wedges a special look by dipping edge in snipped parsley.

Fluted mushrooms: Holding a small sharp paring knife at an angle, begin at the tip of the mushroom cap and carve a strip out of the cap in the form of an inverted "V." Turn the mushroom and continue cutting out inverted "V" strips in a spiral fashion, cutting out a total of 5 to 6 strips.

Tomato roses: Turn the tomato so the stem is down. Begin by cutting a "base" from the tomato (do not sever). Continue cutting one continuous narrow strip (¾ inch wide) in spiral fashion, using a sawing motion, and tapering the end into a point to remove. Curl strip onto its base in the shape of an opening rose.

Onion brushes: Slice off roots from ends of green onions and remove most of the top portion. Make slashes at both ends to produce a fringe. When placed in ice water, the ends will curl back to resemble brushes. For green onion leaves, cut off six inches from tops. Slit one side to open up; cut into ⅛-inch strips from pointed end.

Carrot curls and zigzags: Make thin lengthwise strips of carrot, using a vegetable peeler. For curls, roll up strips and secure with a wooden pick. For zigzags, thread on a wooden pick accordion-style. Place in ice water to crisp; remove picks. Make carrot spirals by rolling a carrot strip and placing it in ice water without a wooden pick.

Chocolate curls and grated chocolate: Use a bar of sweet chocolate at room temperature. Shave curls from the flat surface of the chocolate bar with a vegetable peeler. Use a small-sized hand grater for grating chocolate. Rub the chocolate across the rough surface of the grater to obtain small, fine pieces of grated chocolate.

Appliance Shortcuts

Modern kitchen appliances make cooking more enjoyable and easier than ever. Although certainly not necessary for preparing any of the recipes in this book, the microwave oven and food processor are great aids for quickening many recipe steps. Several general uses for these appliances are described here, so check this page for timesaving hints whenever you begin a recipe.

MICROWAVE OVEN SHORTCUTS	These timings are for micro-cooking at high power. Use heat-resistant or glass-ceramic containers.
Melting Butter or Margarine	Micro-cook 2 tablespoons, uncovered, in glass dish for 30 to 40 seconds.
Toasting Nuts	Spread ¼ cup in a glass pie plate. Micro-cook, uncovered, for 3 minutes, stirring frequently.
Drying Fresh Herbs	Arrange 1 cup fresh herbs, washed, in a single layer on a double thickness of paper toweling. Place a single layer of paper toweling atop. Micro-cook 3 to 4 minutes or till thoroughly dried and crumbly. Store in tightly covered container.
Melting Chocolate	Place unwrapped chocolate squares in microwave oven with folded side of wrapper up. Micro-melt 2 minutes for one square or 2½ to 3 minutes for 2 squares. Lift wrappers by folded ends.
Making Plain Croutons	Spread 4 cups ½-inch bread cubes in a 12x7½x2-inch nonmetal baking dish. Micro-cook, uncovered, 6 to 7 minutes or till crisp and dry, stirring every 2 minutes.
Toasting Coconut	Spread ½ cup flaked coconut in a pie plate. Micro-cook, uncovered, for 3 to 4 minutes or till golden. After 1½ minutes, stir every 30 seconds.
Cooking Onions in Butter	Micro-cook ½ cup chopped onion in 1 tablespoon butter 2 to 3 minutes; stir once.
Cooking Bacon	Micro-cook 4 slices 2½ to 3½ minutes between layers of paper toweling in a dish.

FOOD PROCESSOR SHORTCUTS	Here are directions for processing common foods. The processor is especially helpful when several foods in a recipe need to be chopped or sliced.
Shredded Cheese	Place shredding disk in work bowl. Trim well-chilled cheese to fit feed tube; place in feed tube. Use medium-to-firm pressure with pusher for firm cheeses; use light-to-medium pressure for processed cheeses (4 ounces = 1 cup shredded).
Chopped Hard-Cooked Eggs	Place steel blade in work bowl. Halve hard-cooked eggs; place up to 1 cup halves in work bowl. Process with on/off turns till chopped to desired size.
Chopped Uncooked Meats (beef, veal, pork, lamb)	Place steel blade in work bowl. Remove bone, gristle, and excess fat from meat. Cut meat into 1-inch pieces; place up to 1 cup meat pieces in work bowl. Process with on/off turns till chopped to desired size.
Sliced Leeks	Place slicing disk in work bowl. Trim leeks. Cut into equal lengths about 1 inch shorter than height of feed tube. Place in feed tube, wedging in last one for tight fit. Slice, using medium pressure with pusher (8 ounces = 3 cups sliced).
Chopped Onions	Place steel blade in work bowl. Peel onions; cut into 1-inch pieces. Place up to 1 cup pieces in work bowl. Process with on/off turns till chopped to desired size.
Sliced Mushrooms	Place slicing disk in work bowl. Arrange mushrooms horizontally in feed tube, stacking atop each other to within about 1 inch of top of feed tube. Slice, using medium pressure with pusher (8 ounces = 2½ to 3 cups sliced).
Pureed Berries	Use fresh or thawed frozen strawberries, raspberries, or blueberries. Place steel blade in work bowl; add up to 2 cups fruit. Process till smooth. Strain, if desired.
Chopped Nuts	Place steel blade in work bowl. Add up to 1 cup nutmeats. Process with on/off turns till chopped to desired size (4 ounces = 1 cup chopped).

Index